A Lacanian Conception of Populism

A Lacanian Conception of Populism takes issue with traditional theories of populism, which seek to equate populism with hegemony, arguing that these are not only different but even incompatible logics.

Timothy Appleton contends that one of the main differences between populism and hegemony has to do with the social totality: while hegemony absolutises it, populism eviscerates it, setting in its place an (apparently paradoxical) dispersion of singular instances of 'the people'. The book considers the work of Laclau, Badiou, Žižek and Rancière, before arriving at a novel conceptualisation that Appleton dubs 'the populism of singularities'. In the second half of the book, the author draws out the consequences of this concept for contemporary political theory: the question of how to define 'left' and 'right'; the question of popular enthusiasm and affect; 'truth' versus 'post-truth'; the question of leadership; populism and nationalism; and the relation between populism and political parties.

A Lacanian Conception of Populism will be key reading for academics and scholars of political theory, political philosophy, post-Marxist thought, discourse theory and psychoanalysis. It will also be of interest to those working in the areas of populism studies, cultural studies, gender studies and queer theory.

Timothy Appleton studied discourse analysis with Ernesto Laclau at the University of Essex, before doing a PhD in Philosophy at the Complutense University of Madrid. He is currently a linguistics lecturer at the Camilo José Cela University, Madrid, Spain.

The Lines of the Symbolic in Psychoanalysis Series
Series Editor:
Ian Parker, *Manchester Psychoanalytic Matrix*

Psychoanalytic clinical and theoretical work is always embedded in specific linguistic and cultural contexts and carries their traces, traces which this series attends to in its focus on multiple contradictory and antagonistic 'lines of the Symbolic'. This series takes its cue from Lacan's psychoanalytic work on three registers of human experience, the Symbolic, the Imaginary and the Real, and employs this distinctive understanding of cultural, communication and embodiment to link with other traditions of cultural, clinical and theoretical practice beyond the Lacanian symbolic universe. The Lines of the Symbolic in Psychoanalysis Series provides a reflexive reworking of theoretical and practical issues, translating psychoanalytic writing from different contexts, grounding that work in the specific histories and politics that provide the conditions of possibility for its descriptions and interventions to function. The series makes connections between different cultural and disciplinary sites in which psychoanalysis operates, questioning the idea that there could be one single correct reading and application of Lacan. Its authors trace their own path, their own line through the Symbolic, situating psychoanalysis in relation to debates which intersect with Lacanian work, explicating it, extending it and challenging it.

Psychoanalysis and the Small Screen
The Year the Cinemas Closed
Edited by Carol Owens and Sarah Meehan O'Callaghan

Speculating on the Edge of Psychoanalysis
Rings and Voids
Pablo Lerner

A Lacanian Conception of Populism
Society Does Not Exist
Timothy Appleton

For more information about the series, please visit: www.routledge.com/The-Lines-of-the-Symbolic-in-Psychoanalysis-Series/book-series/KARNLOS

'Appleton's book is much more than just a psychoanalytic interpretation of populism – it is a politically-engaged reading which intervenes in its subject and opens up new ways of emancipatory struggle. To paraphrase the best-known line of Marx: philosophers have hitherto only *interpreted* populism in various ways; the point of Appleton's book is to *change* populist practice itself.'

Slavoj Žižek, *International Director, Birkbeck Institute for the Humanities.*

'Staging an informed, challenging and timely choreography between different strands of contemporary critical political theory (drawing on Rancière, Badiou, Zizek and others), Appleton manages to show populism in a new light. By enlisting psychoanalysis to envisage politics anew, he articulates an original contribution to the Laclau and Mouffe-inspired orientation.'

Yannis Stavrakakis, *Professor of Political Discourse Analysis, Aristotle University of Thessaloniki, and author of* The Lacanian Left *(SUNY)*

'A well thought-out and provocative book on populism which is a must for contemporary debates on the subject.'

Marina Prentoulis, *Senior Lecturer in Media and Politics, University of East Anglia, and author of* Left Populism in Europe *(Pluto Press)*

'Appleton is an original thinker who makes a significant contribution to the field of post-Lacladian theory, inspirational for the understanding of deepening affective hegemonic struggles and populist politics.'

Emilia Palonen, *Lecturer in Politics, University of Helsinki*

'*A Lacanian Conception of Populism* is a book that intervenes in a lucid and original way in today's politico-theoretical scene. It demonstrates the ideological (liberal) bias of those who disdain populist theory, points out the limits of discourses centered on the figure of the proletariat and makes the people of the populist movements the axis of its philosophical reflections. Appleton achieves this aim via a novel and ruptural break with the theory of populism itself: he distances himself from Laclau and Mouffe, abandons the concept of hegemony and, in its place, opts for a populism of singularities *qua* political imagining that is open to the future.'

Luciana Cadahia, *Lecturer in the Pontifical Catholic University of Chile, co-author of* Seven Essays on Populism *(Polity)*

'The political theory of populism is a somewhat impenetrable jungle. Timothy Appleton orientates us and guides us through this terrain, discovering new places for us. The book contains original and interesting ideas about the ideology of populism, the relationship between populism and leadership and between populism and nationalism, and also offers a new vision of the role of antagonism in politics. This work will be an unmissable reference in the debates on populism.'

Ignacio Sánchez-Cuenca, *Professor of Political Science, Carlos III University, Madrid, author of* The Left: End of (a) Cycle *(Catarata)*

A Lacanian Conception of Populism

Society Does Not Exist

Timothy Appleton

Routledge
Taylor & Francis Group

LONDON AND NEW YORK

Designed cover image: © Getty Images

First published in English 2024
by Routledge
4 Park Square, Milton Park, Abingdon, Oxon OX14 4RN

and by Routledge
605 Third Avenue, New York, NY 10158

Routledge is an imprint of the Taylor & Francis Group, an informa business

© 2024 Ned Ediciones

Translated by Timothy Appleton

The right of Timothy Appleton to be identified as author of this
work has been asserted in accordance with sections 77 and 78 of
the Copyright, Designs and Patents Act 1988.

Originally published in Spain as:
La política que viene by Tim Appleton

© 2022, Ned Ediciones

All rights reserved by and controlled through Ned Ediciones

British Library Cataloguing-in-Publication Data
A catalogue record for this book is available from the British Library

Library of Congress Cataloging-in-Publication Data
Names: Appleton, Timothy, author.
Title: A Lacanian conception of populism : society does not exist /
    Timothy Appleton.
Other titles: Política que viene. English
Description: 1 Edition. | New York : Routledge, 2023. | Series:
    The lines of the symbolic in psychoanalysis series | Includes
    bibliographical references and index.
Identifiers: LCCN 2023014288 (print) | LCCN 2023014289 (ebook) |
    ISBN 9781032557205 (hardcover) | ISBN 9781032557182
    (paperback) | ISBN 9781003431916 (ebook)
Subjects: LCSH: Populism. | Political science—Philosophy.
Classification: LCC JC423 .A61713 2023 (print) | LCC JC423
    (ebook) | DDC 320.56/6201—dc23/eng/20230403
LC record available at https://lccn.loc.gov/2023014288
LC ebook record available at https://lccn.loc.gov/2023014289

ISBN: 978-1-032-55720-5 (hbk)
ISBN: 978-1-032-55718-2 (pbk)
ISBN: 978-1-003-43191-6 (ebk)

DOI: 10.4324/9781003431916

Typeset in Times New Roman
by Apex CoVantage, LLC

Contents

Series editor foreword

Lacanian psychoanalysis is a clinical practice but also, in the hands of adepts of radical social theory, has been an influential conceptual resource for political intervention. Indeed, Lacanian psychoanalysis, which emerged from a dramatic break from the bureaucratically ossified mainstream institutions that guarded the theory and practice of the unconscious after Freud's death, has, from the beginning, entailed a form of organisational and political critique. How, Lacan asked, is it possible for an intrinsically questioning approach to subjectivity and social relations to be turned into a tool of adaptation, as it was in the hands of psychoanalysts who, after adapting to their own cultural–political contexts, busily adapted their analysands to society.

Psychoanalysis has rarely been 'popular', though in some parts of the world psychoanalytic discourse did take hold – appearing in commentary and analysis of social phenomena in the mass media – and it is precisely in such contexts that a critical reflection on what 'populism' as such was also developed. In Argentina, for instance, the success and failure of left-wing and right-wing populist political movements have posed a question to psychoanalytically informed social theorists, such as Ernesto Laclau, who is one of the guiding theoretical influences on this book, *A Lacanian Conception of Populism*.

At stake here is the intimate link between unconscious social processes – the very symbolic forms that make us human – and language, language through which an appeal is made to others for recognition and, in political discourse, language as populist rhetoric through which a leader operates as compass point, sometimes as revolutionary leader and sometimes as caudillo. In Lacanian psychoanalysis, many social theorists after Laclau – and here also Timothy Appleton in a finely argued series of interventions into contemporary political discourse – took up Lacan's argument that 'the woman does not exist'; this is a statement that is often misunderstood, and rendered into discussion as if women do not exist at all rather than pointing to the lack of a single defining characteristic of woman, with, Lacan claims, the 'the' rather than the 'woman' being under erasure.

Right-wing communitarian forms of populist political discourse elevate the existence of their conception of society into a quasi-organic taken-for-granted entity, and leaders mobilise their followers to protect that society from those targeted as outsiders. What is symbolic, then, relies on imaginary, ideological conceptions to embed themselves in common sense. To say, as the sub-title of this book does, that 'society does not exist' is to tackle this head-on, and so a Lacanian conception of populism enables us to attend to the structuring of signifiers that comprise the discourses that define society for us. Attention to the symbolic and to the imaginary aspects of political discourse is, then, accompanied by attention to the real of antagonism, the always present, but often ideologically obscured, field of debate that enables challenge and change. This book is thus oriented to left-wing forms of political discourse and to radical politics.

Psychoanalytic clinical and theoretical work circulates through multiple intersecting antagonistic symbolic universes. This series opens connections between different cultural sites in which Lacanian work has developed in distinctive ways, in forms of work that question the idea that there could be a single correct reading and application. The Lines of the Symbolic in Psychoanalysis series provides a reflexive reworking of psychoanalysis that transmits Lacanian writing from around the world, steering a course between the temptations of a metalanguage and imaginary reduction, between the claim to provide a god's-eye view of psychoanalysis and the idea that psychoanalysis must everywhere be the same. And the elaboration of psychoanalysis in the symbolic here grounds its theory and practice in the history and politics of the work in a variety of interventions that touch the real.

Ian Parker
Manchester Psychoanalytic Matrix

Prologue

A new division of the populist sensibility

It is well known that the term 'populism' has been systematically degraded, in the regime of its general circulation. Expelled from the conceptual order of ideas, it has shared the fate of the term 'Machiavellian'. Both now refer to anti-democratic, manipulative excesses that play on the ignorance of the public. It is difficult to save populism from the stigma of madness, just as it is a great challenge to separate Machiavellianism from general cynicism. This is the dominant common sense. However, if there is one thing that is of no interest to Timothy Appleton, it is a received 'common sense'. This is why he, taking theoretical populism as his starting point, has taken the path towards the highly inaccessible space of singularity. In the Appleton I know there is always an ironic approach to common sense, which is where his subtle theoretical sensibility comes from.

Thus we find ourselves, in the present book, confronted by a serious attempt to settle accounts with the aforementioned term. For a long time now, Appleton has concerned himself with the irreverent idea of giving a new value to populism and inscribing it in a theoretical and logical sequence that is different from its usual foundations.

This book is organised, via a highly clear order of exposition, around a convergence of different theoretical folds. While Appleton pays exhaustive attention to the classics of populism, he breaks with an established pact and articulates them with certain communist theorists, thus producing a new theoretical corpus. From his 'populism of singularities', Appleton subtracts the term 'hegemony', which had conventionally been the backbone of the populist hypothesis. Moreover, he refuses to pit 'singular presentation' against the collective efforts of the contemporary communists. The condition of possibility of such an operation is his unorthodox reading of the theory of the subject and of Jacques Lacan's logics of sexuation.

It is for the reader, after having been presented the populist and communist theories with great exactitude, to decode whether the irreducible tension between the void of the subject and the full and contingent presentation of hegemony may or may not be sutured. Here we have a decisive political problem. For Appleton, the presentation of the void neither annuls, nor cancels, the task to come, with its representation in the party or State form.

For years I have participated with Appleton in an impassioned discussion of these matters. This singular book is the highest denouement of that encounter.

Jorge Alemán

Preface to the English edition
Society does not exist

This book is an English translation of one that was recently published in Barcelona, by *NED Ediciones*. Generally speaking, the original text has been translated phrase for phrase into English. However, in the months since the Spanish version of the text was published, it has occurred to me that there is one element in the original manuscript that could perhaps be clarified, or highlighted. Such a manoeuvre seems doubly appropriate since we have employed that element as the subtitle of the English version of the book. I refer to the theorem: society does not exist. The latter is an idea that is formulated explicitly only once or twice in the original text, even though it probably constitutes one of its most original and important aspects. Perhaps the author didn't quite realise this at the time. As our great inspiration for the present work, Jacques Lacan, might have said, here we have an example of the logical time of the subject: it was a retroactive catch. The phrase 'society does not exist' is of course polemical, in part because it immediately threatens to separate left-wing politics (which I would synonymously call *populist*) from 'socialism', even if only in its vulgar form. With this, the ideological paraphernalia of the social link is also defenestrated, to the chagrin, one imagines, of a significant section of leftist thought. The full implications of this move I will leave to one side for the moment, since they are beyond the scope of this book, not to mention, in part, beyond the imagination of its author. Since the idea threatens to prove controversial, however, I feel that it should probably be explained up front.

First, our intention is not to reiterate Margaret Thatcher's notorious comment: 'there is no such thing as society', which can only be understood in its full – i.e. non-axiomatic – form: 'there is no such thing as society, there are only individuals and their families'. If this were a philosophical thesis, we would not accept it, since the idea that it is only individuals (and 'families', whatever they are) that establish a world of meaning is one that we consider completely wrong. A moment's reflection on the existence of the institution of language easily disproves this idea. Next, we come to Ernesto Laclau's almost exactly contemporaneous theoretical argument regarding 'the impossibility of society'. What Laclau meant is that even though meaning is, in a sense, socially constructed, it is never complete. This is why he uses the word impossible. Neither is this our argument, exactly, although, as usual, Laclau begins to point us in the right direction. Finally, one is reminded of Lacan's earlier argument, that 'woman does not exist'. In spite of what some simpletons might think, this does not constitute a sexist remark. All Lacan means by it is that the subjectivity otherwise known as woman – in the abstract sense – has no real existence. All that exists at that level is simply the experience of *women*, in the plural, which is therefore to be understood, in Lacan's telling, one by one. Now, female subjectivity is not, of course, equivalent to a whole society. However, the key point here is the way in which Lacan radically rules out the existence of a tendentially consistent totality, known as woman, in favour of an (apparently paradoxical) plurality of singular experiences of female subjectivity. This, then, is the theoretical idea we feel should be extended to the concept of society. In fact, there is another precedent that one could reference in this regard, which comes from contemporary philosophy. It is not exactly Lacanian, but it perhaps allows us to get a slightly better grip on what is being argued here. I am referring to the 'new realism', or 'realist ontology', of the young German philosopher Markus Gabriel, and his accompanying 'no-world view' (as he calls it). I could add that I consider the realist turn in contemporary philosophy to be the most interesting and important mode of contemporary thought, one to which I think we should be faithful. What is Gabriel's idea?

Gabriel argues that the world does not exist. How does he justify this thesis? His argument is rigorously logical. Perhaps one could reduce it to a syllogism: i) in order for something to exist, it must be located in a field of sense; ii) the world is not located in a field of sense, since it is understood as the space within which all possible fields of sense are gathered together; iii) the world does not exist. Since we are political theorists, instead of philosophers, we shall not speak about worlds, but rather about society. Thus: i) in order for something to exist as a social field, it must be delimited by a political antagonism; ii) society is not delimited by a political antagonism, since it is understood as the space in which all possible social fields are gathered together; iii) society does not exist as a social field. Indeed, since society is normally understood to be a social field, it is possible to abbreviate the latter conclusion, and simply say that society does not exist, which also allows us to capture the Lacanian resonance of the phrase (a resonance that I find to be quite compatible with 'new realist' thought). Perhaps the most important thing that the two arguments share is the assertion of the infinite excess of elements of a totality over that totality itself, which is in fact a slightly more conventional idea, albeit one that is still valid and relevant today. Here I have in mind the infinite excess of inclusion over belonging in set theory.

Such glosses may also help to explain what we take to be the central theme of the present book, namely the separation of populism and hegemony, in order ultimately to do away with the latter. What is our problem with the concept of hegemony? First, for hegemony to exist, an articulation must take place between social fields within an intensional space. Since we do not believe that such a space exists – for, like Gabriel's *world*, if it were to exist, the objects it contained would not – hegemony also cannot exist. Nevertheless, populism, *qua* description of (paradoxically plural) singular antagonisms, in line with Lacan's 'one-by-one' of women, we find to be an entirely valid approach. We conclude that this separation of populism from hegemony – something that, as far as we know, has not been carried out before in social theory, at least explicitly – should now be comprehended under the motto: *society does not exist*. One last thing should be mentioned here: in the English version of the book, I have chosen to include one or two recent essays as appendices. Such are magazine or newspaper articles that, I hope, will slightly help to situate – often at a more political level – some of the theoretical arguments that are set out in the rest of the text.

Acknowledgements

Many people have contributed to the making of this book. First of all, I should like to thank Alfredo Landman and Paula Pons at NED Ediciones, for accepting the first version of the text, and for helping me with it. I should also very much like to thank Ian Parker and Susannah Frearson at Routledge for all their help and support.

There are two people who I feel deserve special mention. First of all, my great friend, the psychoanalyst Estela Canuto. She not only helped me express my ideas in the original Spanish, but she has also accompanied me intellectually throughout the entire writing process. I would also like to thank Jorge Alemán, whose intellectual and personal generosity seems to be limitless. I should also note my admiration for the great theoretical achievements he has obtained during an unparalleled intellectual career. He is perhaps the person who has had the most important political and theoretical influence in my life.

I want to thank all my friends and colleagues at *Cruce Arte y Pensamiento* in Madrid. In the Cruce reading group, we have studied and debated key ideas for more than ten years, and the members' influence on the thesis and methodology of this book has been fundamental. Above all, I thank Zacarías Marco, Noemí Castiñeira, Lorena Pereyra, Amanda Núñez, Javier Rodríguez, Isidro Herrera, Amelia Ruíz, Rosa Jiménez, Simón Royo, Concha García, Daniel Lesmes and José Alberto Raymondi.

I also want to thank my colleagues at *#lacanemancipa: The Magazine of the Lacanian Left*, for their support and inspiration: Julia Gutiérrez, José García Molina, Lidia Ferrari and Fabiana Rousseaux. I must also express my gratitude to our ally Papo Kling for having given (non-)imaginary form to the first version of my argument.

To my friends from Lavapiés, whom I have debated with and antagonised for several years: the important philosopher Rodrigo Menchón, the historian Carlos Cañete and the anthropologist Adolfo Estalella. I also want to mention a colleague and essential interlocutor from my neighbourhood, the brilliant philosopher Carolina Meloni, as well as a great philosopher from another, rather similar neighbourhood: Laura Llevadot.

I thank my two great friends, the philosophers Ignacio Castro and Ricardo Espinoza Lolas, two 'vitalists' who have encouraged me to persevere in all projects, even when it hardly seemed to make sense to do so. It is also impossible not to mention my friend, the young writer Nicol A. Barria-Asenjo, for her vital spirit, and for always proposing new and interesting projects.

I want to thank my two compatriots, friends and, for several years, fellow activists, Alan McGuire and Matt Morgan. Both are graduates, like me, of the hard political school of Corbynism. Our long political talks and meetings within the Labour Party itself have been decisive in my way of thinking about the current political situation.

On the international scene, I should like to thank those that have helped and supported me so much: Yannis Stavrakakis, Luciana Cadahia, Emilia Palonen, Marina Prentoulis, Pablo Bustinduy and Ignacio Sánchez-Cuenca. I consider all of them to be key and fundamental theorists of 'the populist moment'. I would also like to thank my teachers at the University of Essex, from whom I learned so much: Ernesto Laclau, Jason Glynos, David Howarth and Aletta Norval.

I would like to dedicate this book to my doctoral thesis supervisor, Miguel Marinas, who passed away last year. For me, Miguel was the model of the committed and ethical intellectual, as well as being an incredibly generous person, both personally and professionally. I know I'm not the only one who will miss him very much. I would also like to express my gratitude to my family – Sophie, Mum and Dad – for all their emotional, political and material support over the years. Lastly, and most especially, I want to thank my wife, partner and best friend, Abigail Williams, without whom nothing at all would make any sense.

Acknowledgements

Many people have contributed to the making of this book. First of all, I should like to thank Alfredo Landman and Paula Pons at NED Ediciones, for accepting the first version of the text, and for helping me with it. I should also very much like to thank Ian Parker and Susannah Frearson at Routledge for all their help and support.

There are two people who I feel deserve special mention. First of all, my great friend, the psychoanalyst Estela Canuto. She not only helped me express my ideas in the original Spanish, but she has also accompanied me intellectually throughout the entire writing process. I would also like to thank Jorge Alemán, whose intellectual and personal generosity seems to be limitless. I should also note my admiration for the great theoretical achievements he has obtained during an unparalleled intellectual career. He is perhaps the person who has had the most important political and theoretical influence in my life.

I want to thank all my friends and colleagues at *Cruce Arte y Pensamiento* in Madrid. In the Cruce reading group, we have studied and debated key ideas for more than ten years, and the members' influence on the thesis and methodology of this book has been fundamental. Above all, I thank Zacarías Marco, Noemí Castiñeira, Lorena Pereyra, Amanda Núñez, Javier Rodríguez, Isidro Herrera, Amelia Ruíz, Rosa Jiménez, Simón Royo, Concha García, Daniel Lesmes and José Alberto Raymondi.

I also want to thank my colleagues at *#lacanemancipa: The Magazine of the Lacanian Left*, for their support and inspiration: Julia Gutiérrez, José García Molina, Lidia Ferrari and Fabiana Rousseaux. I must also express my gratitude to our ally Papo Kling for having given (non-)imaginary form to the first version of my argument.

To my friends from Lavapiés, whom I have debated with and antagonised for several years: the important philosopher Rodrigo Menchón, the historian Carlos Cañete and the anthropologist Adolfo Estalella. I also want to mention a colleague and essential interlocutor from my neighbourhood, the brilliant philosopher Carolina Meloni, as well as a great philosopher from another, rather similar neighbourhood: Laura Llevadot.

I thank my two great friends, the philosophers Ignacio Castro and Ricardo Espinoza Lolas, two 'vitalists' who have encouraged me to persevere in all projects, even when it hardly seemed to make sense to do so. It is also impossible not to mention my friend, the young writer Nicol A. Barria-Asenjo, for her vital spirit, and for always proposing new and interesting projects.

I want to thank my two compatriots, friends and, for several years, fellow activists, Alan McGuire and Matt Morgan. Both are graduates, like me, of the hard political school of Corbynism. Our long political talks and meetings within the Labour Party itself have been decisive in my way of thinking about the current political situation.

On the international scene, I should like to thank those that have helped and supported me so much: Yannis Stavrakakis, Luciana Cadahia, Emilia Palonen, Marina Prentoulis, Pablo Bustinduy and Ignacio Sánchez-Cuenca. I consider all of them to be key and fundamental theorists of 'the populist moment'. I would also like to thank my teachers at the University of Essex, from whom I learned so much: Ernesto Laclau, Jason Glynos, David Howarth and Aletta Norval.

I would like to dedicate this book to my doctoral thesis supervisor, Miguel Marinas, who passed away last year. For me, Miguel was the model of the committed and ethical intellectual, as well as being an incredibly generous person, both personally and professionally. I know I'm not the only one who will miss him very much. I would also like to express my gratitude to my family – Sophie, Mum and Dad – for all their emotional, political and material support over the years. Lastly, and most especially, I want to thank my wife, partner and best friend, Abigail Williams, without whom nothing at all would make any sense.

Introduction

Populism is dead, long live populism!

'The populist moment is over', declared José Miguel Rojo in his 2018 article in the Spanish newspaper *El Salto*.[1] His opinion was probably representative. He argued that this 'populist moment' had begun in 2011, following the financial crisis, and began to decline when the Spanish political party *Podemos* was incorporated into the municipal governments of Spain.[2] He added that the populist phase ended once and for all in 2018, with the passing of the motion of censure in the Spanish Congress, which removed then-President Mariano Rajoy from his post. Curious, this thesis. After all, if a representative part of the relevant sequence was the meteoric rise of a new political party, *Podemos* (which started in 2014 and by 2015 looked like it was on the point of becoming the second-biggest political party in Spain, even though it ultimately failed to do so), it seems odd to argue that the highest moment in the development of this party (managing to overthrow a sitting government) was also its lowest. Nevertheless, for those of us with memories long enough to contemplate the torpedoing, by the powers-that-be, of Jeremy Corbyn's political project in Britain and that of Bernie Sanders in the United States, it is hard to resist the idea that the populist moment has run out of steam in general, at least in the European and North American contexts. Thus we arrive at a paradox. Ernesto Laclau, the thinker whose ideas have most influenced populist politics in Spain, famously described populism as *ontological*.[3] In other words, he believed that there is something in it that pertains to the general being of politics. How can it be that something that has constituted the history of politics as such can suddenly cease to do so in the year 2018? This contradiction is duplicated in Chantal Mouffe's book *For a Left Populism*, which was published in 2019. In that text, Mouffe describes the overwhelming urgency today of building a populist antagonism that nevertheless constitutes an 'ineradicable' part of all 'human relationships'.[4] It is difficult to see how both analyses can be valid simultaneously. We will return to this paradox in a moment.

It is important to ask what Spanish intellectuals think of their own version of populism because over the last decade, Spain was seen to be the epicentre of this political form. One thinks of the invitations that were extended, during that period, from such venerated publications as *The Guardian* and the *New Left Review*, to the leader of *Podemos* Pablo Iglesias, to outline his 'populist' theories in their pages.[5]

DOI: 10.4324/9781003431916-1

In British intellectual circles, Spain's populist phenomenon may have partly been seen as an extension of its strong tradition of *Eurocommunism*, in the latter part of the previous century. One should refer here to the leader of the Spanish Communist Party, Santiago Carrillo, whose book *'Eurocommunism' and State* had traditionally been considered a fundamental text of that movement.[6] The connection between these two political moments – Eurocommunism and populism – is their shared heterodoxy with respect to classical Marxism, to which one might also add a certain historical tendency in Spain to embrace the political strategy of the popular front. In spite of the prestige in which these traditions are held, however, it is true that the Spanish left has lately tended to mention the word populism less and less, thus handing it over to those who would use it in derogatory fashion. One example of this disdain is the Spanish liberal left, a sector that has traditionally produced a great deal of anti-populist propaganda. Here one could cite the leader of the *PSOE*, Pedro Sánchez, who is currently president of the Spanish government. In 2014, Sánchez commented that: 'The destiny of populism is the Venezuela of Chávez, poverty, ration cards, a lack of democracy and, above all, inequality.'[7] Perhaps we can conclude, then, that the 2020 electoral pact between the *PSOE* and *Podemos* verifies José Miguel Rojo's thesis, mentioned at the outset. The immersion of the celebrated Spanish populism in parliamentary processes has limited it for the moment, at least as a discursive strategy for the Spanish radical left.

The first people to precipitate this shift may have been *Podemos*' academic allies. For example, it is quite surprising that, in his book *In Defense of Populism*, from 2016, the Spanish philosopher Carlos Fernández Liria does not actually present anything that could reasonably be described as a defence of populism, but rather refers to the latter as an unfortunate but necessary bridge to the author's main political goal, namely, a cosmopolitan republic.[8] An identical tendency is seen in an early domestic advocate of *Podemos*, top Spanish philosopher José Luis Villacañas. In his 2015 book *Populism*, Villacañas concludes thus:

> Republicanism shares some features with populism, but above all it is an autonomous, ancient and respectable political tradition, in respect of which populism represents a massive simplification. However, what will end up deciding between them will be the material basis of society itself, not the theoretical or rhetorical capacity of one or the other.[9]

Once again, the argument is that the correct political goal is republicanism, but sometimes, due to a complicated social situation, the vehicle in order to reach it is going to have to be populism. One could ask, with friends like these, who needs enemies? Personally, I would say that there is a family resemblance between the arguments of Liria and Villacañas and the liberal critique of populism (by figures like Pedro Sánchez): both liberalism and republicanism are based – theoretically – on the idea of a fundamental social consensus, which populism, whose starting point is the opposite, social division, wishes to undermine decisively.

An interesting phenomenon at this level is the tug-of-war between Spanish and Latin American intellectuals. The presence of populist politics throughout Latin America is well known, but a key country on this score is Argentina, wherein the phenomenon was first properly theorised, probably due to the enduring presence of Peronism in that territory. Many consider Peronism to be the paradigm of this political form. Two important references in this regard are Ernesto Laclau, who is really the most important modern theorist of populism, and Jorge Alemán, who has extensively developed Laclau's ideas. In fact, it could be argued that these two thinkers have had more influence on the populist sequence in Spain than Spanish intellectuals themselves, in part due to their insistence on supporting its eponymous term. For my part, I agree with this insistence, and I feel that the fact that I am English is not an accident in this respect. I mention this because over the last few years, populism has experienced a relative revival in the Anglo-Saxon world. In what sense?

Almost all the important presenters of new left online media, in countries like the United States and Great Britain, now describe themselves as 'populists'. For example, the most developed left-wing online platforms in the two countries, *The Young Turks* in America and *Novara Media* in Great Britain, have published articles with titles such as: 'If the fake populist Trump can win, imagine what a real populist could do'; and 'Is populism the new punk?'[10] Another key example would be the major online political show, *The Hill*. Its erstwhile presenters, Krystal Ball and Saagar Enjeti, jointly published a book at the beginning of 2020 in which they speculated that the next phase of politics in the United States will essentially be populist. The title of the book summed up its main idea: *The Populist's Guide to 2020: A New Right and a New Left Are Rising.*[11] Another important literary reference – this time from Britain – would be the 2019 book by prominent *Novara Media* journalist Aaron Bastani: *Fully-Automated Luxury Communism*, in which the author conjectures – paradoxically, perhaps – that the political form that the new mode of communism he promotes will assume will be that of populism.[12] 'Luxury populism', he calls it. Finally, one finds a range of independent left voices in the U.S., like those of Jimmy Dore, or Kyle Kulinski, who frequently appear to consider populism an isomorphic description of the kind of radical politics that they favour.[13] In other words, the Anglophone world has begun to extol this term at the very same time that the countries of southern Europe, such as Spain, have started to distance themselves from it. Nevertheless, and bearing in mind my personal relationship with the Spanish-speaking world, I like to think that this new wave of Anglophone populism partly reflects the influence of movements like *Podemos* and also of Argentine theory. On the other hand, one should probably recognise that it has always been less controversial to defend populism in English-speaking countries than in the rest of the world, Spanish-speaking territories included. Why?

Margaret Canovan, in her book *The People*, has hypothesised that the English-speaking world is more comfortable with the term populism because the word 'people' is more versatile in English than in other languages. In our tongue, it can either be an abstract noun (*people*) or a concrete noun (*the people*).[14] In Spanish, to give only one example, you have to use two different words to capture these two meanings (*gente* and *pueblo*). Canovan argues that this bivalence in the English term means that it simultaneously denotes potentiality and actuality. Along the same lines, in Anglophone cultures the people is seen not only as something excluded (and therefore, a threat), but also as the legitimate basis of any constitutional system. Such arguments would perhaps require further discussion, but one could speculate that this linguistic aspect in itself justifies the description of populism as ontological in the oeuvre of Ernesto Laclau (who worked for much of his life in England). Perhaps it is appropriate to mention that the etymology of the very word 'populism' is English. The *People's Party* began in the United States at the end of the 19th century, and the word 'populists' seems to have been used colloquially to refer to its members and representatives.[15] A final relevant factor here could be the fact that Marxism – which is a partial rival of populism – has never been an especially influential system of thought in the Anglophone world. American author Thomas Frank puts it the following way: 'Reduced to its essence, populism is the way Americans express class antagonism'.[16]

To paraphrase Mark Twain, perhaps we can say that rumours of the death of populism have largely been an exaggeration. Does this mean that I consider that classical populist theory is still valid? In some ways yes, but I think that it needs to be modified with regard to one important point, which is the main task of this book. What is the innovation I propose? The Argentine–Spanish nexus has long assumed that the concept of populism is practically synonymous with that of hegemony. To put it in the words of Iñigo Errejon, one of the most important 'organic intellectuals' from the first phase of *Podemos* (although he has now left the party), and someone who has been greatly influenced by Laclau's work:

> populist discourse is that which unifies highly diverse positions and social sectors in a dichotomization of the political field that opposes the traditional elites to the 'people' *qua* construction, through which the subaltern sectors successfully demand the representation of a forgotten or betrayed general interest.[17]

In other words, populism necessarily involves a hegemonic operation. My position is completely different. I will argue not simply that there is a tension between hegemony and populism but that they in fact represent fundamentally incompatible logics. Why?

First, one must point out the shared element between hegemony and populism. Both depend on the category of *social antagonism*. According to authors such as Laclau (and his collaborator Chantal Mouffe), the condensation of particular signifiers in a hegemonic bloc depends on the presence of a 'constitutive outside', while populism, for its part, depends on a dichotomy between the people and the elite. However, I would say that the status of antagonism is different in the two theories. Essentially, it seems to me that in the case of populism, we are faced with a *radical* antagonism, whereas in hegemony, such antagonism is *mediated*. I have in mind the way in which a populist antagonism constitutes a singularity, while hegemony oscillates – in a way that I consider inviable – between the singularity and plurality of antagonisms that can be found in a social formation. Why do I describe this approach as inviable? If, as the theory of hegemony says, an antagonism is what *constitutes* such a social formation, it is perfectly impossible – as the theory itself asserts – for this formation to incorporate further antagonisms, because this would mean that it also encompasses further social formations, which would represent a contradiction. I believe that one effect of this contradiction is a certain indecisiveness on the part of its purveyors regarding the antagonistic moment itself, which renders infinitely difficult the political militancy that is supposed to accompany this mode of thought. Since we are not writing a mystery novel here, I shall set out without further ado the denouement of my own argument: I will resolve the aforementioned theoretical blockage not by ruling out the possibility of multiple antagonisms (a proposition I fully accept) but simply by concluding that a social formation is not an appropriate category within which to capture them.

I consider this conclusion to be a variation on the Laclauian thematic of the impossibility of society, although I feel it is a more complete version of it.[18] Perhaps at this point we could take a first leaf from the book of Lacan. In the same way as, in 1973, Lacan had averred, without any irony whatsoever, that 'woman does not exist', perhaps we should now say that society does not exist. In fact, I think it is no accident that the Laclauian formula must be updated today, since the last such update precipitated a whole new phase of politics, which is what I feel is also at stake today. Here I have in mind the apparent discovery by Slavoj Žižek, published in 1987, that the category of antagonism in Laclau and Mouffe could be considered a politico-theoretical version of Lacan's psychoanalytic concept of the *real*.[19] One also recalls Žižek's caveat: Laclau and Mouffe had not fully developed the very concept they were responsible for hatching. Žižek's explanation for this theoretical underdevelopment echoed Stalin's notorious judgement on the failure of his collective farms policy: 'dizziness from too much success'. Perhaps, then, it is time to repeat this diabolical complement, and speculate that a similar attack of dizziness is what explains the problems associated with the otherwise innovative – and crucial – Laclauian idea of the impossibility of society. As Sade might have put it: 'one more effort if you would prove that society does not exist!'

I feel that one important effect of this conclusion is that it solves one of the most tediously insistent dilemmas of the contemporary left, by which I mean the interminable debate over whether issues of identity or those of economy should take political precedence. An example of this confusion is the melancholy bestseller *The Diversity Trap* (*La trampa de la diversidad*), by Spanish author Daniel Bernabé. Bernabé's argument is that we should recognise that the fundamental struggle of a social field is that of the economy, in relation to which all other struggles should be considered epiphenomenal. To reiterate, this conclusion seems fallacious to me not because of its apparent political bias, but because it is based on a false conception of the social space within which the dilemma supposedly arises. It could be added that, although the theory of hegemony officially stands in opposition to Bernabé's thesis – since according to it no specific struggle can or should be privileged above all others – I believe that this theory ends up duplicating the error, since it necessarily condenses multiple antagonisms into one, within a supposedly unified social field. The deduction I shall make from all this is that populism, with its emphasis on the absolute singularity of an antagonism (yet without limiting a priori the number of fields within which such might emerge), is the only logic that is truly capable of embracing what I would call the fundamental 'dispersivity' of what we usually refer to as a social order. Furthermore, I believe that this conclusion is valid regardless of the moment in which it is deployed, which solves the problem of anachronism, mentioned at the beginning of this Introduction. A further advantage of my argument, I believe, is that it avoids the opposite error to that of Bernabé. What do I mean by this?

The opposite mistake, I think, is to try to avoid potential problems with the category of antagonism by *softening* it. A pertinent reference here is Chantal Mouffe, with her concept of *agonism*. According to Mouffe's way of thinking, political activists have an obligation to militate for an antagonism, on condition that they simultaneously recognise their enemy's right to do the same. It's probably best not think about the Kantian dilemmas that a formulation of this type threatens to produce! Indeed, such an idea is in fact rather traditional. It echoes the mythical Voltairian phrase attributed to Evelyn Beatrice Hall: 'I disagree with what you say, but I will defend to the death your right to say it'. In the case of Mouffe, I would add that her position is a side effect of the theoretical problems associated with her conception of hegemony. In other words, I see her ambivalence about antagonism as a result of the fact that hegemony presupposes a social space, of determinate extension, that could be filled with progressive forces. If one starts from this premise, it is logical that the two fundamental antagonists one finds in this space (the people and the elite, say) will both be fully constituted, in exactly the same way as will be the set that encompasses them. In such a context, it is true that the only option for these antagonists would be to compromise on their demands, for if they were not to do so, they would inevitably fall into all-out war. So, how might this problem be solved? Once again, my answer would be: by unmaking the relevant social set. One way to perform this task would be that which we mentioned before: emphasising its dispersivity. However, there is a further solution that could be mentioned here (even if its status in relation to the first solution is rather complex).

First of all, it should be noted that Mouffe's concept of antagonism is highly influenced by the work of controversial German legal theorist Carl Schmitt. Schmitt argued that in politics, there are two fundamental categories: friend and enemy. According to him, this distinction is parallel to that of beauty and ugliness in aesthetics, good and evil in morality, and profitability and unprofitability in economics.[20] I would accept this idea. Nevertheless, I can see why it might cause offence: it seems to refer to the kind of blind antagonism one finds in, for instance, Samuel Huntington's 'clash of civilizations'. After all, it must not be forgotten that Schmitt was a member of the Nazi Party in Germany. To avoid this difficulty, then, I once again propose to supplement the reference to Schmitt with one from Jacques Lacan. I believe that when we think of Schmitt's distinction, we must consider it in terms of Lacan's theory of sexual difference, i.e. as a radically imbalanced division, in which one part is constituted and the other is, so to speak, utterly deconstituted (an idea that reflects the distinction between the feminine and masculine position in Lacan's formulae, of which more later). The effect of this Lacanian conception is that one side of an antagonism will be invisible from the point of view of the other. This conclusion thus also decentres once and for all the social set that incorporates the two antagonists, which should remove any anxiety around the idea that the latter constitute perfectly formed entities.

I have already said that one of the fundamental thinkers of populism and hegemony is Ernesto Laclau. The first chapter of this book, then, will focus on his theories, which were partly elaborated with Mouffe. At the same time, we will identify what we consider to be the internal obstacles of such theories. In order subsequently to overcome such obstacles, I feel it is necessary to go through the debates between Laclau and other post-Althusserian thinkers.[21] Above all, we will contemplate the division between those who advocate neo-populism (among whom I would include Ernesto Laclau and Jacques Rancière) and those who, in contrast, defend neo-communism (Alain Badiou and Slavoj Žižek). This argument will be another way of discussing the clash between the singularity and the plurality of antagonisms, which we mentioned earlier on. An important element of our ruminations will be the fact that Laclau himself has commented on the work of each of the other authors I propose to include. Laclau's comments will therefore guide us, up to a certain point, through the discussion. At the end of our reflections, we will end up closest to Rancière's position, but at the same time we aim to clarify some of its more obscure (even, obscurantist) aspects and supplement it with important ideas that come from the arguments of the other authors we have covered. Once this process has been carried out, and our theoretical premises established, we will try to identify some key theoretical consequences that have to do with more general debates around populism. I have chosen six such issues to deal with: i) the question of whether populism should ultimately be considered a left-wing or a right-wing phenomenon, ii) the question of popular enthusiasm, iii) the question of truth versus post-truth, iv) the question of leadership in populism, v) the question of the relationship between populism and nationalism, and vi) the question of the attitude that populists should maintain towards political parties.

Notes

1 www.elsaltodiario.com/camara-civica/se-acabo-el-momento-populista-en-espana.
2 The phrase 'populist moment' comes from Chantal Mouffe, *For a Left Populism* (London: Verso), 2018.
3 See: Ernesto Laclau, *On Populist Reason* (London: Verso), 2005.
4 Chantal Mouffe, *For a Left Populism* (London: Verso), 2019, pp. 90–91.
5 www.theguardian.com/politics/2015/dec/15/podemos-pablo-iglesias-jeremy-corbyn-spain-election-radicalism-labour; https://newleftreview.org/issues/II93/articles/pablo-iglesias-understanding-posemos.
6 Santiago Carrillo, *Eurocomunismo y estado* (Barcelona: Crítica/Grijalbo), 1977.
7 www.europapress.es/nacional/noticia-sanchez-avisa-fin-populismo-venezuela-chaves-cree-pp-frota-manos-auge-20140910215917.html.

8 Carlos Fernández Liria, *En Defensa del Populismo* (Madrid: Catarata), 2016, p. 203.

9 José Luis Villacañas, *Populismo* (Madrid: La Huerta Grande), 2015, p. 119.

10 www.youtube.com/watch?v=urDxXyq7jYA; https://twitter.com/novaramedia/status/84 7115867318108160.

11 Krystal Ball and Saagar Enjeti, *The Populist's Guide to 2020: A New Right and a New Left Are Rising* (Washington: Strong Arm Press), 2020.

12 Aaron Bastani, *Fully-Automated Luxury Communism: A Manifesto* (London: Verso), 2019, p. 188.

13 E.g. www.youtube.com/watch?v=KO_xj03C3aA; www.youtube.com/watch?v=-OP5O LBauCg&t=567s.

14 Margaret Canovan, *The People* (Cambridge: Polity), 2005, pp. 19, 105.

15 Although another important etymology is Russian, care of the Narodniki (populist, in Russian) movements, in the late 19th century.

16 www.theguardian.com/books/2018/may/23/thomas-frank-trump-populism-books.

17 Iñigo Errejón and Chantal Mouffe, *Construir Pueblo: Hegemonía y radicalización de la democracia* (Barcelona: Icaria), 2016, p. 87, author's translation.

18 Ernesto Laclau, *New Reflections on the Revolution of Our Time* (London: Verso), 1990, pp. 89–92.

19 Slavoj Žižek, Beyond Discourse Analysis, in: Ernesto Laclau (Eds.), *New Reflections on the Revolution of Our Time* (London: Verso), 1990, pp. 249–260.

20 Carl Schmitt, *The Concept of the Political* (Chicago: University of Chicago Press), 2007, p. 26.

21 I say post-Althusserian because all the relevant writers were disciples of the French 'structuralist Marxist' Louis Althusser.

Part I

Chapter 1

Populism versus hegemony

It is surely reasonable to describe the most recent phase of left-wing politics as populist, at least in the West: one thinks of the so-called Pink Tide in Latin America (and its contemporary revival), *Podemos* in Spain, Jeremy Corbyn in Great Britain and Bernie Sanders in the United States.[1] We can think of two justifications for this description. First, this type of politics has traditionally been 'formally' antagonistic to the social status quo; this is something we consider to be a fundamental characteristic of populism. Second, the sequence in question has been intellectually overdetermined by post-structuralist political theory, whose apogee was precisely the concept of populism, in the works of thinkers such as Ernesto Laclau and Chantal Mouffe. However, even the most optimistic person would have to admit that the upward trajectory of left-wing populism – at least outside Latin America – seems to have been interrupted, for the time being. Does this imply that we should abandon it as a political paradigm? It seems to us that it would be rash to do so, in part because we consider that it has proved a highly productive moment in contemporary politics and also because, and partly for the same reason, we believe that it may well be reactivated in the future. On the other hand, the fact that we are experiencing a pause in the story of contemporary populism should perhaps be taken as a sign of something. How should we interpret the lacuna? We believe it requires us to re-examine the theoretical premises of the movement, in order to consider whether they are still completely valid. This is the task we will try to accomplish in what follows. By the end, we will come to a simple but important conclusion. We believe that if we want to continue to consider ourselves populists, it will be necessary to dissociate populism from the theory of hegemony, which until now has practically been considered its synonym. How did we arrive at this conclusion?

The preceding idea is the product of our reading of the debates within the theoretical generation that has most influenced the recent phase of radical politics: the post-Althusserian thinkers. It should be noted straight away that not all of these authors can be considered to be 'populists'. Some refer to themselves as 'communists'. However, it seems to us that it is useful to take seriously the 'communist' critique of 'populism' at this level, not in order to renounce the last term, but precisely in order to clarify its theoretical basis. In the following pages, then, we will summarise our analysis of these debates. First, we will discuss the concept of

DOI: 10.4324/9781003431916-3

populism that arose primarily from the work of Ernesto Laclau (and which then continued to be developed by Chantal Mouffe) and contemplate its connection to the concept of hegemony; next, we will consider the work of Alain Badiou, which is somewhat similar to that of Laclau but introduces points that go beyond the latter's position and will help us greatly with our task of rethinking populism; then, we will see how Slavoj Žižek develops some of the same points as Badiou and goes one step further than the latter in terms of our consideration of populism, even if he has not yet completed the task we consider decisive; finally, we will examine the important synthesis of all these innovations, which we believe can be found in the work of Jacques Rancière. Before closing, we shall try to refine one or two aspects of Rancière's work, and then draw several conclusions from the theoretical path we have travelled up to that point. We suspect that this will help us with the very precise question of how we should think about, and do, politics in the coming period.

Laclau

Populism in Laclau's early work

Ernesto Laclau's first book – *Politics and Ideology in Marxist Theory: Capitalism, Fascism, Populism* – is based on Marxist theory and especially influenced by the work of the French Marxist Louis Althusser. One of Laclau's central preoccupations – as his title suggests – is populism, and the book represents a highly original take on how Marxism might tackle the topic. The rumour at the University of Essex, where Laclau worked, was that after publishing his first book, he wanted to write a longer treatise on the question, but in the end this second tome was postponed, and he began preparing another, with Chantal Mouffe, that would make both authors famous. We are referring to *Hegemony and Socialist Strategy: Towards a Radical Democracy*, which came out in 1985, and whose fundamental theoretical issue was – predictably – that of hegemony. The question of populism does not arise in this second book, nor in those that followed it. In the end, Laclau's definitive text on the subject was his final one, *The Populist Reason*. When this last book ultimately came out, however, Laclau's treatment of populism was completely imbued with his now-celebrated theory of hegemony, almost as if the two concepts were identical. Nevertheless, we must also recognise that the Gramscian dimension of hegemony was already present in Laclau's first book. How so?

In *Politics and Ideology . . .*, Laclau discusses – as do many Marxists – the class elements one finds in a particular mode of production. Above all, he is interested in the distinction between the proletariat and the bourgeoisie under capitalism. The fundamental part of his argument consists of separating the Marxist concept of mode of production from what he calls a *social formation*. He believes that each contains a different contradiction. He associates mode of production with the contradiction between classes, and social formation with the contradiction between the people and what he goes on to call the 'power bloc', which later on he referred to – as do other analysts of populism – as *the elite*.[2] Another term that Laclau uses to describe the enemy of the people is *the state*.[3] In fact, this second kind of contradiction – between the people and the elite – is an example of what Mao Zedong would have called an *antagonistic* contradiction, and Laclau considers the dimension of antagonism that it contains to be a fundamental aspect of politics. It is in this sense that he describes the people as a 'democratic' force. What Laclau is essentially saying is that a class contradiction should not be considered political in itself, an idea that is echoed later in his 1990 essay *New Reflections on the Revolution of Our Time*, in which he argues that a contradiction is an objective factor, while politics as such involves an essentially subjective dimension.[4] His fundamental intuition here is that a class position is somehow inert until it transcends itself, precisely at the point when it finds itself articulated with a 'social' struggle. This, then, is the Gramscian part of Laclau's early argument, in the sense that it involves a transformation of, and relationality between, distinct elements within a social field.

One point must be emphasised here. The antagonistic dimension of politics, which Laclau associates with populism, is not only fundamental but also represents an excess. In what sense? In his first book, Laclau speaks of the continuity of a people, in the face of the historical discontinuity that is associated with class elements.[5] Like the distinction between mode of production and social formation, he considers this difference to be radical. From this we can deduce the irreducibility of a people with respect to history as such. It could even be said that Laclau sees 'the people' as a historical remainder, in the same way that Hegel separated certain peoples from universal history (albeit with the opposite political implication).[6] This 'excessive' dimension of the people is probably what led Laclau, in his final book, to describe populism – now understood in terms of the political production of the people – as an *ontological* aspect, in the sense of something that infinitely exceeds what Heidegger calls onticity (regional being). In sum, for Laclau, populism can be considered the irreducible framework of any political experience whatsoever.

These two aspects – politics as antagonism, *qua* ontological factor – are reflected in the works of several recent theorists of this issue. They can be found in Chantal Mouffe's 2019 book, *For a Left-Wing Populism*, which is indeed conceived as a continuation of Laclau's work. Mouffe states that:

> Laclau defines populism as a discursive strategy of constructing a political frontier dividing society into two camps and calls for the mobilization of the 'underdog' against 'those in power.' It is not an ideology and cannot be attributed a specific programmatic content. Nor is it a political regime. It is a way of doing politics that can take various ideological forms according to both time and place, and is compatible with a variety of institutional frameworks.[7]

Once again, populism – that is, antagonism – is seen as the *form* – separated at a minimally infinite distance from its *content* – of all politics. The same two aspects can also be found in the recent definition of the term populism in Jan-Werner Müller's bestseller on the subject. First of all, Müller speaks about anti-elitism and anti-pluralism, two aspects that define his vision of political antagonism; when he adds that populism is a very vague doctrine, he evokes its second aspect: formality.[8] Two other experts in the field, Cas Mudde and Cristobál Rovira Kaltwasser, in their *Populism: A Very Short Introduction*, had already anticipated the description provided by Mouffe: 'we define populism as a *thin-centered ideology that considers society to be ultimately separated into two homogeneous and antagonistic camps, "the pure people" versus "the corrupt elite"*'.[9] Again, we find here a reference to the antagonistic aspect, while the term '*thin-centered*' expresses the infinite providence of said antagonism.

It has already been explained that the theoretical gesture in Laclau that produced these conclusions is that of the autonomy of a social formation.[10] If the latter were not autonomous, its antagonistic division would not be radical. However, this idea poses some problems. The first is the fact that in his inaugural book, Laclau undermines, at a certain point, the irreducible character of populism, precisely by placing it in a relation to the class question, which he describes as 'determinant in the last instance' of social struggles (thus evoking Althusser's formula, as derived from Engels). This introduces an insurmountable tension in his argument. Laclau exacerbates this tension when he adds that what we call socialism describes the moment when the figure of the people is completely hegemonised by the working class. This puts Laclau's Leninist heritage on full display, since he is here in line with Lenin's famous theory of the vanguard class (which, incidentally, is also present in Gramsci). Laclau's conclusion in this regard is striking:

> *In socialism, therefore, coincide the highest form of 'populism' and the resolution of the ultimate and most radical of class conflicts.* The dialectic between 'the people' and classes finds here the final moment of its unity: there is no socialism without populism, and the highest forms of populism can only be socialist.[11]

It is true that this clash – between the autonomy of social formation on the one hand and its lack of autonomy on the other – begins to be resolved in Laclau's second book, *Hegemony and Socialist Strategy*, when its authors decisively distance themselves from class determinism (an argument that we will consider in the next section). It is also true, however, that if Laclau had managed to solve this problem satisfactorily from the beginning, he would have precipitated another. Which one?

In a certain sense, the second problem that arises from Laclau's argument is the opposite of that which we have just outlined. That is to say, if, in his first book, he had been able to fully develop his own thesis regarding the autonomy of the people – thus freeing the latter from the class determinism associated with conventional Marxism – he would have given rise to another type of determinism: that of a social formation. Of course, what Laclau nominally wants to do is to decentre such a formation, by excluding the people from it (although the latter is still present *qua* potentiality), but this does not affect the fact that it contains only one type of fundamental demand: that which is directly opposed to the state understood as a unity. This 'totalisation' of antagonism would therefore make it into a zero-sum game, which is supposedly what Laclau's whole project seeks to avoid (and would also undermine his famous Gramscianism). In short, the more the early Laclau radicalises the figure of the people, the more he undermines that very radicalisation. What a dilemma! The goal of the rest of this chapter is to solve both problems. To do so, we must begin by exploring in detail how Laclau and Mouffe tried to resolve the first of them, through their elaboration of the theory of hegemony. We can say in advance that we will accept and adopt much of their argument with regard to this problem. However, we believe that accepting their preliminary solution makes a second step even more urgent, a step that we shall try to take – without the help of Laclau – later on.

Populism and hegemony

Laclau and Mouffe's theory of hegemony comes from their deconstruction of the history of Marxism. Their argument at this level is that the history of the concept of hegemony reflects the growing importance of what they call the realm of the *contingent*, within the Marxist horizon.[12] The contingent in what sense? As is often the case in their theoretical approach, it has a twofold structure (there is an ambiguous double movement in almost all of Laclau and Mouffe's theoretical arguments). First, it has to do with the pluralisation of elements within the social space. The second aspect is the specific character of the political leadership that must be exercised in such a context. Laclau and Mouffe see these two points as a challenge to the traditional Marxist thesis – which can be seen in, for example, the *Communist Manifesto* – regarding the simplification of the social structure, according to the 'necessary laws' of history. To explain all of this, it will first be necessary to summarise the critical genealogy provided by Laclau and Mouffe.

Laclau and Mouffe's genealogy of Marxism (in the Nietzschean sense) begins with the Second International. Two key examples from this period are Eduard Bernstein and Georges Sorel. Laclau and Mouffe argue that Bernstein's 'revisionism' was the first movement in the history of Marxism to take seriously the pluralisation and diversification of the social sphere. With regard to Sorel, they argue that when he interpreted the proletarian revolution as a general strike, he ended up emphasising the *symbolic* dimension of politics, now separated from the economic base of society, which according to traditional Marxism was the cause of its simplification and solidification. Later on, Laclau and Mouffe discuss the so-called political voluntarism – which has sometimes been described as opportunism – of Lenin, which allowed him to take advantage of the unforeseen political situation in Russia, in the second decade of the 20th century, in order to energise and precipitate the communist revolution. Specifically, Laclau and Mouffe explain how Lenin tried to combine more than one political struggle: that of the incipient industrial proletariat in Russia and also that of the peasants, together with an incomplete liberal-bourgeois revolution. As the authors note, this is actually the first version of the 'permanent revolution' thesis, an idea that Trotsky invented (even though he retroactively projected it onto Lenin). The moment of contingency here is specifically related to what Trotsky once called 'Unevenness, the most general law of the historic process'.[13] It is true that this aspect brought contingency into the very heart of political history, because it implied, once again, the simultaneity of divergent political struggles, on the one hand, and, on the other, the subsequent moment of construction – which must be understood as radically contingent and, according to Laclau and Mouffe, contains an irreducibly symbolic component – within which these struggles are combined. According to Laclau and Mouffe, the pinnacle of all these efforts to think the (contingent) unity-in-plurality of political struggles is Gramsci's theory of hegemony. For the latter, all possible social classes are united through the leadership – 'hegemony', in the etymological sense – of the proletariat. If the theory of hegemony can already be found in Gramsci, however, what exactly does Laclau and Mouffe's theoretical innovation consist of? Its originality seems to lie in removing the last remaining 'necessary historical laws' from this theoretical picture. How did they do this?

Deploying a variation on Gramsci's theory, Laclau and Mouffe argue that there is no particular class that is historically destined to play the leadership role in a movement for social change, not even the proletariat in the context of a capitalist society. Again, they reach this conclusion partly because they consider history to be an open process, without *telos*, but also because they emphatically reject the associated Marxist premise of a simplification of social space, which would logically reduce the number of candidates that could assume a leadership position within it. Laclau and Mouffe argue – partly on the basis of sociological evidence – that in reality what has taken place is a *complexification* of said space (according to what they see as the conditions of late capitalism) and a concomitant increase in the pluralisation of struggles. They even hypothesise that the proletariat in the classical sense no longer exists, or if it does, it does not constitute anything like a nodal point in the series of emancipatory struggles that are taking place today. Despite reaching this conclusion, however, the authors accept much of the morphology of Leninist theory, as described previously. For example, they believe that leadership – hegemony – has to exist, in politics. Why do they think so? Couldn't they simply posit a sheer dispersion of elements, within a social space?

Laclau and Mouffe think that an absolute fragmentation of social elements would eliminate the dimension of contingency as radically as would the doctrine of historical necessity. They come to this conclusion because they consider that contingency represents a certain decentring of the social body, and if this body is thought of as completely dissected, paradoxically it would once again constitute a centred totality, since the relationship between its many elements would somehow be considered stabilised. Another way of expressing this idea is via Laclau and Mouffe's comments on the French Revolution. According to them, said revolution was the last moment in which a pure political antagonism could be experienced in the social field. However, they add that in the social dispersion that followed it, the egalitarian and universalist horizon that the French Revolution formalised remained omnipresent. They conclude that in all the new political struggles of today, it is a matter of applying this egalitarian logic, which they also refer to as 'democratic'. Essentially, they consider that the preeminent task of politics today is to extend democracy to a growing number of social realms. Again, we are dealing here with a hegemonic logic. In order to formalise their conclusions, Laclau and Mouffe supplement their reading of the history of Marxism with their interpretation of (post-)structural linguistics. How have they interpreted this 'movement'?

The most important thing Laclau and Mouffe retain from (post-)structural linguistics is the idea that language has two fundamental axes. The linguist Roman Jakobson – a key reference in this field – has identified these axes as *metaphor* and *metonymy*.[14] Why these two? The argument runs as follows. According to the structuralist tradition, language consists of a series of differences between signs. This thesis is based on the internal arbitrariness of the sign itself, i.e. that its two parts – the signifier and the signified – are not intrinsically connected. Hence Ferdinand de Saussure (the involuntary founder of structuralism) concludes that what gives 'value' to the sign is its difference from other signs. But there is a complication. If language consisted of nothing more than a series of differences, the arbitrariness of the sign would be abolished, since a mutually exclusive series would be a complete series, and in such a context the relationship between the signified and the signifier would again be isomorphic (and the basic structuralist thesis – of the fundamental disconnection between them – would collapse). A clear parallel can be seen here with Laclau and Mouffe's analysis of the history of Marxism: both arguments demonstrate that there is more than one way to abolish contingency in a system. Again, then, we find ourselves obliged to conclude that the series of differences proper to language must be subverted at a certain point. The most common way of theorising this subversion is in terms of what is opposed to difference: *similarity*, which could also be called *identity*. The two axes of Jakobson, then, correspond to the distinction between difference and identity: metonymy equates to difference and metaphor equates to identity. What Laclau and Mouffe propose is that we interpret these two axes in political terms. The result of this is their distinction between *equivalence* (metaphor) and *difference* (metonymy). Here a key question arises in relation to our argument. Where does *antagonism* fit into the theoretical picture we have just described?

At times, it seems as though the concept of antagonism in Laclau and Mouffe is fully compatible with the findings of (post-)structural linguistics, since it seems that the correlate of the latter, in the political field, is the categories of equivalence and difference. On the other hand, difference understood as a *system* of differences (in the plural) – an idea that forms a fundamental part of the structuralist horizon – cannot be the same mode of difference as that presented in a social antagonism, because the latter is necessarily univocal and is, therefore, according to Laclau and Mouffe, the limit of all social objectivity. Hence, what one finds in Laclau and Mouffe's category of antagonism is *difference against difference*: radical difference versus metonymic difference, so to speak. This is why Laclau and Mouffe end up associating antagonism with the dimension of *equivalence*, mentioned earlier. This conclusion therefore situates antagonism fully within the theory of the two axes of language: for Laclau and Mouffe, antagonism is the other side of metaphor, or equivalence.

T_s

D_1

D_1 D_2 D_3 D_4

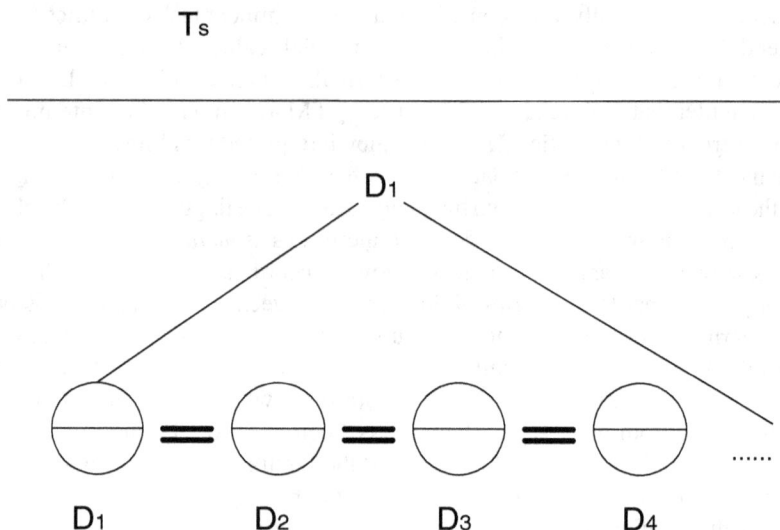

Figure 1.1 Hegemony according to Laclau.

All of these factors are diagrammatised in a late Laclau essay, 'Constructing Universality' (and later in *The Populist Reason* itself) (Figure 1.1).

In this diagram, antagonism is represented by the bar, which distributes the 'radical difference' between the enemy – Tsarism in the diagram (hence, the 'Ts'; Laclau is using the example of the Russian Revolution here) – and a principal demand (D_1) that converts other differential demands (D_1, D_2, D_3, D_4, etc.) into equivalents.[15] In this sense, D_1 is the hegemonic signifier. Thus we have the three aspects already mentioned: metonymic difference (D_1, D_2, D_3, D_4, etc.), equivalence (D_1) and radical difference, or antagonism (between D_1 and Ts). The example of the Russian Revolution might also remind one of the debt that Laclau and Mouffe owe to Marxism.

Earlier we commented that at a certain point, Laclau (and later Mouffe) combines this theory with that of populism. How does he do so? We have already explained the idea that Laclau considered populism to be the most direct expression of politics as such, i.e. infinite social antagonism. Given everything that has been explained in this section about Laclau and Mouffe's theory, then, we can now make a clear deduction: for these authors, populism represents the antagonistic dimension of hegemony itself. In this sense, the D_1 in Figure 1.1 represents the people against its perpetual enemy: the elite. This conclusion is important because it implies that there is no populism without hegemony, and vice versa. Immediately after reaching such a resounding conclusion, however, the problem that we cited at the end of the previous section comes back with a vengeance: according to this theory, how does one avoid a totalisation of antagonism, within a given social formation? Before answering this question, one must first ask, how is it that the problem arises in the first place?

The theoretical difficulty here is quite straightforward: Laclau and Mouffe are contradicting themselves. How so? First of all, according to Laclau's position, within a social space (Figure 1.1, for instance) there are various demands, which then combine to form an antagonism. At first glance, this logic seems impeccable. However, it is fallacious. In order to explain why, we must first point out that *stricto sensu*, each of these demands represents an antagonism in itself. Is this a fair statement? After all, in *The Populist Reason*, Laclau clearly states that a demand must be seen as the 'atomic unit' of an antagonism, thus appearing to separate out the two aspects. However, if this were really the case, then what would be the ontological source of such demands? The only possible such source is a social schism. But we already have a name for this phenomenon: antagonism. To prove the point, we can carry out a basic symptomal reading of Laclau's text: in his diagram, he also describes the 'primary antagonism' as a demand (D_1). In other words, in spite of what he says, it is ultimately Laclau himself who does not recognise the logical distinction between demands and antagonisms. It must be said that Laclau and Mouffe were in fact more consistent on this point in their earlier book, *Hegemony and Socialist Strategy*. Therein, they stated:

> when we have spoken of antagonism, we have kept it in the singular in order to simplify our argument. But it is clear that antagonism does not necessarily emerge at a single point: any position in a system of differences, insofar as it is negated, can become the locus of an antagonism. Hence, there are a variety of possible antagonisms in the social, many of them in opposition to each other.[16]

The clarification is appreciated. However, the argument remains flawed. Why? Simply because antagonisms cannot 'contain' other antagonisms. If that were the case, then what the authors call 'the social' would itself collapse, since what defines it is an antagonism and nothing else. In other words, if it is true – as Laclau and Mouffe argue in another moment – that antagonism is the limit of all (social) objectivity, the earlier quote would imply that one can have one 'limit of all objectivity' within another 'limit of all objectivity', which would make no sense at all.[17] These conclusions now allow us to fully understand the problem of totalisation that we discussed earlier on: it is a problem because it is based on an insoluble contradiction.

We would like to clarify straight away that we are not saying that Laclau and Mouffe are wrong in pluralising the possible number of antagonisms. At this point in history, this thesis seems to us to be frankly irrefutable. What we are questioning is simply their way of combining this idea with the construction of a single social formation. How, then, can the problem of the apparently simultaneous existence of plural and singular antagonisms be solved? Let us now turn to the other post-Althusserians. We have already listed them: Alain Badiou, Slavoj Žižek and Jacques Rancière. In fact, the debate between these thinkers and Laclau is real, in the sense that Laclau has written explicit critiques of the theoretical projects of all the authors mentioned. In the following sections, then, as well as reflecting on the theories of each of these thinkers, we shall also consider, at the end of each part, Laclau's comments on their respective projects. This, we hope, will allow us to keep our dialectic on track. We start with the work of the French philosopher Alain Badiou. Badiou is important in the first place because he appears to resolve completely the contradiction between singular and plural antagonisms that is found in Laclau and Mouffe. He does so simply by privileging singularity. We should add that in the process, he draws an entirely different political conclusion to Laclau and Mouffe: he ends up defending communism (*qua* singularity), rather than populism. As we will see later, however, Badiou ultimately does not solve the general problem we are discussing here, although we feel that he does provide the first clue as to how to do so. To consider his position on the subject, we must first describe his specific 'ontology'.

Badiou

Badiou's theory

There are two fundamental categories in Badiou's philosophy: *situation* and *event*.[18] To understand them, one has to consider the starting point of his ontology (that is, his theory of being *qua* being). This point is summarised in the following phrase: 'the One is not'. What Badiou deduces from this principle is that what *is* is multiple. However, he recognises that 'there is something of the one' (to use the phrase he borrowed from the psychoanalytic theorist who has influenced almost all the key authors we are dealing with in this chapter, Jacques Lacan). What he means by this is that there do exist unifying effects within the fundamental multiplicity of being. These effects produce what Badiou calls a *situation*. At another point, he calls it the 'count-as-one'. He adds that there is a kind of multiplicity that is perfectly compatible with this moment of unification. He calls this 'consistent multiplicity'. He contrasts it with 'inconsistent multiplicity', which is the element that he considers truly ontological. Since this second type of multiplicity is completely invisible from the point of view of a situation, Badiou connects it to the *void*. He thus concludes that the void is the true name of being. According to him, the void is produced because in inconsistent multiplicity, each multiple is in fact a multiple of multiples. This means that within the fundamental multiplicity of being, each multiple can be decomposed into other multiples, *ad infinitum*. Since the void, when considered in this way, in fact threatens the stability of each situation, another element is introduced, which Badiou calls 'the state of the situation'. What is this and why is it important?

For Badiou, the state 're-presents' the consistent multiplicity of the situation, in order that the latter may be consolidated. In principle, it does so in order to protect a situation from its own void, but in reality, all it ends up doing is limiting the 'excess' of this situation, rather than its void. The term *excess*, for Badiou, describes that type of multiple that is not included in a situation but does indeed belong to it. In other words, it is a question of multiples (which Badiou calls *elements*) that are apt to be subordinated to the state but that as yet, and contingently, are not. The void, on the other hand, is found in multiples (which Badiou calls *parts*) that are included in a state but do not belong to it (by definition, because they are empty). Badiou calls this second type of multiple a *singularity*. Another name he gives it is 'the eventual site', since it is the terrain on which an *event* can later be built (although this process will not necessarily take place). To express it in Badiou's terminology, the event is a multiple that 'subtracts' itself from the count-as-one of a situation, by adhering to its void. It could be added (since it will later prove important) that Badiou here introduces the category of the *subject*, which for him is precisely the 'agent' of an event, a role that this subject is obliged to assume, since its very existence depends on that of an event. Moreover, according to Badiou, there are four different types of events, which are formed by subtracting oneself from four different types of situations: artistic, amorous, scientific, and political. We are focusing, of course, on the last of these categories. Examples of political events that Badiou has provided are: the French Revolution, the Russian Revolution, the Chinese Cultural Revolution, May '68 in Paris, the Iranian Revolution and the 'Solidarity' movement in Poland in the 1980s. These examples show that for Badiou, politics (like all events) is fundamentally perturbing. In part, the explanation for this is the coincidence between the ontological term 'state', in Badiou, and a political state. For Badiou, any true politics must withdraw from the state in the traditionally political sense. Hence, politics, for Badiou, is necessarily a revolutionary affair.

The key aspect of this theory of the event from the point of view of our argument is that for Badiou, there can only be one event in each situation. This doesn't mean that the course of an event is in any sense predictable. It merely implies that whatever this course is, it will partly be determined by its adherence to the void of a specific situation. In his more recent works – especially *The Logics of Worlds: Being and Event 2* – Badiou has tried to qualify the theory that we have just described, by introducing the category of *world*. In this new theory, Badiou hints that within a world there could be diverse phenomena that are not completely reducible to a particular situation.[19] However, upon reading the text carefully, one discovers that in fact a world is isomorphic with a situation. From this one can deduce that the world in which an event is found is also singular (despite its apparent internal diversity). So, if we assume (as we must) that an event in Badiou equates to antagonism in the sense of Laclau and Mouffe, this would imply that Badiou has resolved the contradiction found in the work of the latter authors, a contradiction that we pointed out at the end of the previous section. He appears to have done so by decisively opting for one of its two sides: absolute singularity. Here one could ask a supplementary question. In our earlier discussion of Laclau and Mouffe, we commented that these authors reject the Marxist hypothesis of the continuous simplification of social space. If they are right, does Badiou's idea of the singularity of an eventual site therefore involve a return to classical Marxism?

Unlike traditional Marxism, Badiou's thesis does not imply a 'teleological' view of history. Badiou does not believe that the class struggle between the proletariat and the bourgeoisie is the *final* struggle, which, at the moment of its consummation, is going to bring about the end of history. In this way, one could add, Badiou is attempting to maintain the rawness of antagonism at all times. In fact, part of his disagreement with Marxism is that he considers that, ultimately, the latter wants to *reduce* antagonism, since it sees it as a merely regional phenomenon in the unfolding of a totality: a Hegelian error, for post-Althusserian thinkers such as Badiou (along with Laclau, who has made a very similar critique of Marxism).[20] As has already been mentioned, Badiou's fundamental philosophical axiom is 'the One is not'; this means that for him, there is no totality to be unfolded. A political consequence of this ontological argument is that, in contrast to the Marxists, Badiou (at least in his slightly earlier work) does not aim to *abolish* the state, as would supposedly be the case in a communist society. What he prefers to do is maintain an 'principled distance' towards it.[21] This is what would ensure the continuation of the antagonism that for him – like Laclau and Mouffe – defines politics.

Despite these differences with regard to classical Marxism, it is clear that a situation in Badiou's sense will be absolutely simplified in the very moment that an event is separated from it. Perhaps that is why Badiou continues to defend communism, as an alternative to the capitalist world in which we currently live. This, plus the singularity of events, implies that it is difficult – perhaps impossible – to differentiate Badiou from classical Marxism in directly political terms. It does not seem at all accidental that the only book by Marx that Badiou cites with any regularity is *The Communist Manifesto*, since this early text by Marx represents the basic version of the thesis of the absolute simplification of social space, plus a defence of its communist 'supplement'. In the same way, when he has to speculate regarding the privileged subject of today's politics, Badiou increasingly returns to the same term – the *proletariat* – and insists that the political project of this class must be called *communism*. How would he defend himself against the accusation, which arises from Laclau and Mouffe, among others, that the classical proletariat no longer exists (at least in the West)?

Badiou seeks his proletariat wherever he can. His most recent formulation is that it has assumed nomadic form and will come from the Third World and land in the West. He even goes so far as to describe this group as a 'vanguard class'.[22] He speaks, for example, of the workers who travel from Korea, Nepal, Bangladesh, Morocco, Mali etc. Are such groups really about to bring about a communist revolution? To us, this seems doubtful. Indeed, Badiou's idea almost seems to us to represent a theoretical regression, with respect to classical Marxism. At least the Marxists of yesteryear were very clear about where they could find an 'evental site': in the factories of their own countries. Despite these reservations, perhaps Badiou can at least boast of having resolved the theoretical contradiction found in Laclau and Mouffe's work, between the singular and the plural. But in truth, even this is not entirely the case. Badiou's work also contains a contradiction, and – curious to say – it is the same as was found in Laclau and Mouffe's work. Where do we find it in Badiou? Ironically, the person who identifies it is Laclau himself.

Laclau versus Badiou

In 2004, Laclau published an article – *An Ethics of Militant Engagement* – in which he discusses the ethics proposed by Badiou. The ethical part of Badiou's theory has to do with the fidelity of a subject to an event. In his text, however, Laclau criticises Badiou for certain theoretical inconsistencies that he believes arise in the latter's work. Which ones? We have already explained that according to Badiou, there is no common measure between an event and the situation from which it is subtracted. Laclau says that this is a mistake. For Laclau, it would be better to say that the two elements 'contaminate' one other (to use his own phrase).[23] Why? Let us quote Laclau himself: 'the event is only constructed through chains of equivalences linking a plurality of sites'; next, he states: 'social agents share, at the level of a situation, values, ideals, beliefs, etc. that the truth, not being total, does not put entirely into question' ('truth' being the singular product of an event, according to Badiou's theory); finally, Laclau asserts that:

> The subject is only partly the subject inspired by the event; the naming of the unrepresentable in which the event consists involves a reference to an unrepresented within *a* situation and can only proceed through the displacement of elements already present in that situation. This is what we have called the mutual contamination between situation and event.[24]

It is obvious what Laclau is trying to do here. Once again, he is trying to pluralise the points at which an antagonism could emerge, within a hypothetically unified social space. We have already explained that this idea is unacceptable to us. One wonders: what does the set of 'the plurality of sites' (or 'elements that are already present in a situation') consist of? What does a 'social agent', or 'the subject', consist of, if it is indeed true that all such factors pre-exist the antagonism that theoretically constitutes them? However, putting aside, for the moment, the problems with Laclau's argument, his criticism of Badiou does raise an important question regarding the latter's project: how does Badiou think about the diverse political struggles we indisputably see emerging today?

Badiou's answer to this question would probably be straightforward; we assume he would reiterate that there is only one type of subject: the proletariat. As we have seen, this idea is based above all on his idea of the singularity of such a subject. It could be added that Badiou mistrusts the abstract pluralisation of subjects. In his book *Saint Paul*, when he talks about the new social movements, he does so negatively, since he associates them with the functioning of the capitalist economy. He comments that: 'The capitalist logic of the general equivalent and the identitarian and cultural logic of communities or minorities form an articulated whole'.[25] Perhaps we could ask Badiou a more direct question: what would he do with, for example, the feminist struggle? Would he also describe it as 'proletarian'? Again, one assumes that the answer would be affirmative. This may jar a bit, but on the other hand we must acknowledge Badiou's intellectual consistency with regard to this point. He almost never speaks of feminist struggle as such, and thus avoids talking about the apparent incongruity of his position. On the other hand, avoiding a problem by ignoring it probably has its limits as an intellectual strategy! One might also ask about the relatively diverse examples of historical subjects that Badiou provides in his work. To refer only to the list of political events that we included in the previous section, what do the Iranian and the Russian revolutions have in common? It is true that they share a family resemblance, but they have very different forms. They are not simply anti-capitalist events, which would concern a monolithic proletariat. Nevertheless, we must assume that Badiou would assimilate them to what he identifies as the proletariat, *qua* privileged name of the subject that is excluded from all situations, regardless of their nature. Which, to repeat, makes sense. For us, however, the real limit of Badiou's argument – and this is why we consider Laclau's criticism of him to be important – lies in his use of the term *state* (of the situation). Why do we consider this concept to be problematic?

We believe that the word 'state', in Badiou's project, is a problem because it represents the moment when his 'social ontology' (illegitimately) overdetermines his philosophical ontology. What do we mean by this? First of all, we have seen that, for Badiou, an event (an antagonism) emerges in the ambit of a singular situation. It is equally logical, then, that the state that this situation represents is also singular. But here there is a complication, because a state is usually associated with a unique and exclusive social formation. In this sense, we are forced to conclude that there is not more than one subject of emancipation at not only the theoretical level but the 'factical' level as well. Now, we have conceded that Badiou is consistent on this point. He believes that there is only one subject of emancipation in any circumstance: the proletariat. On the other hand, we believe that this antinomic connection between the proletariat and any conceivable form of state threatens to undermine the most original dimension of Badiou's project: his embrace of the pure contingency of a social formation (and the concomitant irreducibility of antagonism). We would therefore conclude that through his use of the term *state*, Badiou ends up falling into the same trap as Laclau: that of social totalisation. Nevertheless, it must be recognised that the two thinkers are not identical in this regard. As we have seen, Badiou insists that an antagonism is a singularity, and we believe that this is a necessary step to get out of the overall dilemma we are faced with here. We should add that we feel there are few contemporary authors who have thought with such rigour, and in such detail, the wiles of singular antagonism as Badiou. Hence, we shall return to his theorisations in later chapters. In order to continue our attempts to resolve the contradiction of antagonism, however, we must now consider the work of another important neo-Marxist thinker: Slavoj Žižek.

Žižek

Žižek's theory

Žižek is perhaps one of the most prolific philosophers of the day. He appears to publish a major new book every few months. Curiously, however, we believe that many important premises can be found in the 11 pages of his first essay (that was successful at an international level): 'Beyond Discourse Analysis'.[26] We will use this text, then, as the starting point for our summary of his theory. His object of study in the piece is, once again, the book *Hegemony and Socialist Strategy*, by Laclau and Mouffe. Žižek begins by identifying the key achievement of this text as the category of antagonism itself, which, according to him, constitutes a socio-political version of *the real*, which is a key element in the theory of Jacques Lacan (Žižek considers himself a 'dogmatic Lacanian'). Next, he does his own symptomal reading of Laclau and Mouffe, saying that their central innovation in the book was so radical that even they were not able to draw out all of its consequences. The main aspect that Žižek believes the authors have missed is the *subject*. What is the connection that Žižek perceives between the subject and antagonism?

It must first be remembered that Laclau and Mouffe interpret antagonism as the limit of all social difference (in the structuralist sense) and therefore the limit of any society. Žižek believes that the same logic applies to the subject; he argues that it is essential to distinguish, on the one hand, what he calls 'subject positions', which are mutually differentiated within a structure, and on the other, the subject under-stood as the *limit* of said structure. Since Laclau and Mouffe, in their book, define the subject in terms of subject positions, they end up ignoring, according to Žižek, this more radical dimension of subjectivity. The other aspect that Žižek believes that Laclau and Mouffe have overlooked is the theory of the *object*, specifically that object whose emptiness reflects that of the subject to which it corresponds. This is what Žižek calls – again following Lacan – the *object a*. Here it should be noted that these criticisms by Žižek are perfectly valid with respect to *Hegemony and Socialist Strategy*, but later on Laclau – under the influence of Žižek himself – introduces the category of the subject and the object (*qua object a*) into his project, as we shall see later on.

One can already imagine that the concept of the subject *qua* 'bearer' of antago-nism that Žižek presents makes such a subject absolutely singular, unlike the plu-rality of subjective positions found in a social structure. Are we once again dealing here with an 'ontological tension', of the type found in Laclau and Mouffe: that of the apparent simultaneity of the singular and the plural in a single social space? We are not. For Žižek, the subject is not simply something that leads and condenses other elements in a series but is rather a pure void: 'lack', he will call it, which is the Lacanian term. He adds that this dimension of lack is precisely what gives the subject its uniqueness: it is not reducible to any existing element. Žižek will add that the fundamental social antagonism in our capitalist societies is class strug-gle, in the Marxist sense. For this reason, the privileged name of the subject of antagonism, in his work, is currently the *proletariat*. This also explains why he considers himself to be a communist thinker (as does Badiou). Žižek's ultimate political proposal is ineluctable; it is *the dictatorship of the proletariat*. One of the scandalous aspects of this idea is that it is difficult to imagine a more ortho-dox Marxist position. Therefore, we must pose Žižek the same question that we asked Badiou: what is it that separates your ideas from those of classical Marxism?

Like Laclau, Mouffe and Badiou, Žižek does not believe in the necessary laws of history and their counterpart: the thesis of the end of history (in a communist society). He agrees with those other authors that social antagonism is irreducible. However, rather than perceive this as an anti-Hegelian position – as some other post-Althusserians do – Žižek argues that the first version of this argument can in fact be found in Hegel himself. This is something genuinely new in Žižek's project: he describes Hegel as the first 'post-Marxist'.[27] This movement produces a further original aspect of Žižek's work: his innovative interpretation of dialectical materialism (which in truth emanates from his reading of Hegel). What is this interpretation?

Žižek associates 'Marxist philosophy' with a *parallax view*, that is, the apparent change in position of an object when viewed from two different perspectives. This concept invokes Heidegger's ontological difference (between the ontological and the ontic levels), now adding the idea of a radical asymmetry between its two sides (a thought that is derived from Lacan). The constitutive change of perspective that takes place in a parallax view establishes a 'relation-of-no-relation' between the two sides of an antagonism, and this also allows Žižek to theorise a kind of 'transition' between them, under the condition that they pass through a *torsion*. This potential implication between the two sides of a political antagonism (which is based on ontological difference) is reflected in the 'curvature of space' that one finds in a Möbius strip, which can be considered a key theoretical figure for Žižek. If you follow said strip, you will end up in the same position as you were in at the beginning of your journey, but the other way up. This gives a good idea of a political process, according to Žižek's theory.

Another effect of this interpretation of the Marxist dialectic is Žižek's renewed interest in political economy. What does he say on the topic?

It seems that what Žižek is seeking to do here is to rethink the – parallatic – immanence of the economy to politics. He even projects this viewpoint onto Marx himself, saying that in the latter's work, politics and economy always represented a parallax.[28] The idea here is that economics has an 'objectal' status within the field of politics, precisely in the sense that it constitutes a parallax; here we have in mind the Lacanian *object*, which we mentioned previously. In other words, in the parallax, the object *qua* void produces radically contingent subjective effects. If Žižek sees economics as a parallax object, this explains how he can conclude that the *sine qua non* of true politics today is the critique of political economy; essentially, he

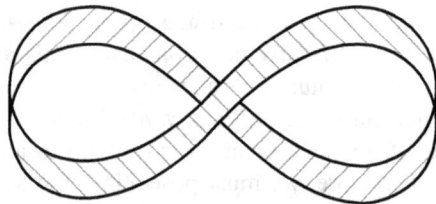

Figure 1.2 Möbius strip.

believes that if we want to do politics nowadays, it will be necessary to deal with some non-political element, namely the economy. This last point again emphasises the *processal* dimension of politics, which is what Žižek really wants to draw out. Its result is supposed to be, once again, the dictatorship of the proletariat. Do such ideas really separate Žižek from Marxism? Once again, they can be considered a nuancing of traditional Marxist theory. The only exception is the idea of the omnipresence of antagonism, which Žižek shares with the other authors we have dealt with so far here, and which is irreducible to Marxist thinking. On the other hand, it is – as it was with Badiou – difficult to imagine the practical importance of this last idea, especially if the end result of it is the traditional Marxist formulation, the dictatorship of the proletariat. Here we might ask, again, how Žižek expects to defend himself against Laclau and Mouffe's charge that the proletariat, as conventional Marxism conceived it, no longer exists.

In his more recent works, Žižek has attempted to radicalise the category. He has listed in several places what he considers to be the 'contradictions' of contemporary capitalism. Normally, he mentions some version of the following phenomena: the environmental crisis, problems with biogenetics, problems with intellectual property, struggles over raw materials, food and water and, finally, growing social segregation. Žižek has argued that all these factors lead to proletarianisation. But what kind of proletariat does he suppose is formed as the result of such processes? Žižek answers that there are proletarians: 'where there are subjects reduced to a rootless existence, deprived of all substantial links'.[29] Again, we see that for him, the subject as such – now understood as the proletariat – is essentially empty. Therefore, he believes that the term proletarian could actually describe any actor, regardless of their social class (on condition that they participate in a revolutionary struggle). This seems to open the door to a major generalisation of the category. For us, the most relevant aspect of this conclusion is that by presenting it, Žižek is trying to rescue, once again, an absolutely *singular* social category. In fact, his position is very similar to Badiou's at this level, which is not a surprise if one considers that Badiou has had a decisive influence on Žižek's work. If this is the case, however, then why have we cited Žižek in our argument? What does he add to the debate that couldn't already be found in Badiou? Before answering, let's first consider Laclau's criticism of Žižek.

Laclau versus Žižek

Laclau's opinion of Žižek is straightforward. He opines that the latter represents a reheated version of traditional Marxism. He accuses him of turning the economy into a transcendent condition of all historical change, rather than a single element in a chain of hegemonic equivalence, which might function as an overdetermining factor, although Laclau would add that this is not necessarily the case and, in the present social context, certainly is not. As Laclau puts it:

> The truth is that the economy is, like anything else in society, the locus of an overdetermination of social logics, and its centrality is the result of the obvious fact that the material reproduction of society has more repercussions for social

processes than do other instances. This does not mean that capitalist reproduction can be reduced to a single, self-defining mechanism.[30]

Is this line of criticism fair? We have already conceded that Žižek reduces all antagonisms to only one: that between capital and labour. We have also explained that this is problematic because it represents a totalisation of the social field. On the other hand, we have added that Laclau makes the same mistake, even if it is under the aegis of hegemony. In this sense we can at least thank Žižek for having tried to resolve the contradiction between singularity and plurality in the theory of hegemony, since he opts – as does Badiou – for absolute singularity. But we believe that there is another important aspect of Žižek's project that Laclau overlooks, namely its topological dimension. Why do we consider this aspect to be so important?

What is interesting about this element is first of all the fact that it leads Žižek to rethink the issue of the state. How so? Here it is interesting to note that, unlike Badiou, Žižek sometimes defends the state politically, up to and including an integral state. Why? First, it should be noted that in his writings, Žižek dramatically multiplies the number of points at which politics can occur. He gives very diverse examples of it, from the Russian Revolution to Richard Nixon's decision to open diplomatic relations with China in 1976; in another moment, he points to the 'evental' character of the referendum on abortion in Italy in 1974, or he celebrates Barack Obama's medical reforms in the United States.[31] It is clear that not all these examples are directly opposed to the state in the sense that, for example, Badiou conceives of it. On the other hand, it is true that they can be considered singularities, in Žižek's terms (since each clearly breaks with a prevailing logic). We assume that what Žižek is doing here is to separate a situation of being from the state as such. This would be the only logical way in which he could defend political singularities and the uniqueness of the state at the same time. It can be speculated that what he really intends to do is turn the state into a kind of transcendental backdrop (to recycle Laclau's term), thus facilitating a dialectic between this element and certain singular struggles, a dialectic that would thus incorporate all the twists and inversions that we talked about before, i.e. the topological dimension.

One can see how this movement promises to resolve aporias that we have found in Laclau (and Mouffe) and Badiou, especially in the latter. Despite its originality, however, it is difficult to see how Žižek might ultimately acquit himself of the accusation of social totalisation. What's more, he could be accused of making the problem worse. Perhaps this is why he ends up oscillating between defending a very local and specific politics on the one hand and something as monolithic as the dictatorship of the proletariat on the other. Indeed, the Hegelian dimension of his theory probably aggravates the problem. In short, if we adopt the position of Žižek, perhaps we will avoid certain paradoxes, but we will nevertheless end up caught in others. Despite this conclusion, we must say that Žižek is the first thinker, of those whom we have discussed so far, who is able seriously to contemplate something that we consider fundamental to the rest of our argument, namely, an (apparently paradoxical) *plurality of singularities*. Nevertheless, we believe that in order to develop this insight further, it will be necessary to put aside the dialectical perspective and move on to a related but different project: that of the post-Althusserian/ post-Marxist thinker Jacques Rancière.

Rancière

Rancière's theory

Rancière shares several of the premises that have been discussed so far. First of all, he believes that politics is essentially antagonism. He calls it *disagreement* and considers that it occurs between a *subject* and what he calls *the police*.[32] He conceives of the latter as the agent of a process in which all the spaces and places that constitute the social order are distributed. The objectivity of this order explains why he believes that the group that opposes it can be considered a subject. The most general name Rancière uses to describe this subject is *the people*. He believes that before the moment in which this people mobilises politically, they remain a *mute* element; he calls it 'the part that has no part'. When this element is declared, Rancière considers that it is presented as a *singularity*, precisely in the sense that it does not conform to any (policed) distribution of social roles. Its equidistance from all such roles also explains why he considers it to be *universal*. He adds that politics involves setting out and testing a hypothesis of *equality*, again in the sense of a separation from the inequality that characterises a social formation. Rancière also uses the word *democracy* to denote the political community that is produced at the point when the part that has no part begins to militate. He calls it 'a community of division', since it is based on the fundamental disagreement that is politics.

It will have been noted that politics, as Rancière conceives it, does not lie in a mere objective binary opposition, but in a questioning of the *limits* of such opposition. That is why he describes it as a 'supplement' with respect to the social-police order. In this sense, he believes that politics implies a distinction between two different worlds: a real one, in which the people are mute, and a hypothetical one, in which the mute people finds its voice and thus demonstrates that it is the equal of any other social segment (it is in this sense that Rancière speaks of a hypothesis of equality). He argues that politics establishes a simultaneous relationship and non-relationship between these worlds (which evokes Žižek's take on ontological disequilibrium). Another way of saying this is when he describes politics as not only a dispute but also a dispute over the very existence of a dispute. This idea of generating another political scene also explains why Rancière focuses on the 'performative' dimension of politics; he conceives antagonism, for example, as a 'speech act', adding that in the same sense, politics will have to be 'staged'. At another point, he talks about the 'aesthetic' dimension of politics. Now, the reader may ask themselves, why do we consider Rancière's theoretical intervention so important? First, let's compare it in more detail with the proposals we already have on the table.

Rancière's thinking is partly compatible with that of Laclau and Mouffe. Like them, Rancière speaks of the people and associates the latter with social antagonism. He also underlines, as Laclau does, the empty character of this people: mute, he calls it (even though, as we have already explained, Laclau and Mouffe hesitate a little over this point). Now, this reference to the people has the effect of distancing Rancière from Badiou and Žižek, who see the proletariat as the essential subject of politics. It is true that Rancière often speaks of the latter class, but he never argues that it is the only name of the subject of politics. Perhaps it could be concluded that for him, the proletariat is one iteration, among others, of the people. Returning to Laclau and Mouffe, it must now be said that despite their similarities to Rancière, there is also an important discrepancy between them: Rancière does not associate politics with hegemonic leadership. The key issue here is that Rancière does not at any point defend the idea that politics implies a condensation of demands, whose only common property would supposedly be that of being 'against the system'. He states that:

A 'people' . . . is not an assemblage of social groups and identities. It is a polemical form of subjectification that is drawn along particular lines of fracture, where the distribution of leaders and led, learned and ignorant, possessors and dispossessed, is decided.[33]

The explanation for this discrepancy is simple (although its implications are not): Rancière does not believe in a 'system' as such, beyond that imposed by the police, and we do not know – a priori – what the latter consists of. As we have seen, Laclau and Mouffe do believe in a system, albeit aporetically: they argue that there is something they call 'the social', which they consider to be filled in later on with specific (and plural) content. Their argument is therefore incompatible with Rancière's insistence on the absolute singularity of a political movement. Does this finally position him closer to Badiou and Žižek, who also do not admit hegemony as part of their respective systems?

Starting with Badiou, it could be noted that there are many parallels between his theory and that of Rancière (which is perhaps unsurprising, given that they partly share a history of political activism in France). There are even moments when Rancière appears to accept elements of Badiou's mathematical ontology, especially when he speaks of a 'counting' (which sounds a lot like the count-as-one of a situation, in Badiou) of 'parts' (the multiple?), in which what he calls 'a part that has no part' (the site of the event?) is repressed. Furthermore, Rancière, like Badiou, clearly distinguishes between the *void* of a 'social' order, a void that in itself is something inert, and its *supplement*, namely politics as such (which Badiou would call an event). Another thing these two authors have in common is that they believe that politics is not ubiquitous; according to Rancière, believing such a thing would be one of the quickest ways to abolish it. Both Rancière and Badiou have said that politics is 'rare', since for each of them, the split between two worlds, which we spoke of earlier, always remains a potentiality until a political subject emerges that is capable of taking responsibility for it. This is another way of saying that they both believe in the absolute singularity of a political sequence. In this sense, it is logical that hegemony, which Laclau and Mouffe theorise, should not be part of their respective projects; in some way, the latter theory would imply that there is a political struggle that is constantly underway: that of filling the void of 'the social'. These, then, are the similarities between Rancière and Badiou. What are the differences?

While both Rancière and Badiou believe in the singularity of an antagonism, Rancière seems to emphasise that such antagonism can emerge from any 'social' point. That is why it includes examples of politics that Badiou would never cite. Rancière mentions, for example, 'an election, a strike, a demonstration'.[34] In this shortlist one finds very different types of political mobilisation. What do parliamentary, trade union or street politics have in common? In principle, little. Rancière has also spoken, on several occasions, about the feminist struggle. There are even times when he raises the possibility of a politics that takes place in what might be considered a *bourgeois* space, which is something that many Marxists would consider an oxymoron.[35] Thus, he ends up producing lists of historical political subjects such as this one: 'citizens, workers, women, proletarians'.[36] The inclusion of proletarians, here, indicates that Rancière does not rule out the possibility of a revolutionary anti-capitalist politics, although once again, we should insist on the fact that he does not consider it to be the only possibility.

These conclusions almost seem to bring us back to Laclau and Mouffe and their early attempt to completely empty out the 'necessary' laws of history proposed by classical Marxism. Again, however, we believe that Rancière is more faithful to this principle, since Laclau and Mouffe seem to defend a social limitation to this process of emptying (via the theory of hegemony), and Rancière does not. Rancière concludes that: 'The heterogeneity of language games is not an inevitability for contemporary societies that suddenly comes and puts an end to the great narrative of politics. On the contrary, it is constitutive of politics'.[37] If we return for a moment to Badiou, it must be said that he also does not believe that politics has an 'ontological' component that could limit it. For this reason, he describes the event, which is the core of his intellectual project, as 'everything-that-is-not-being-*qua*-being'. On the other hand, when Badiou begins to speak of the state, it seems to us that his ontological theory somehow sabotages his non-ontological theory (of the event), thus producing a contradiction. In addition, this means that for him, certain types of politics are ruled out in advance. In this sense, it can be concluded that Badiou, like Laclau and Mouffe, ends up 'substantialising' the supposed emptiness of a 'situation'. We believe that Rancière does not make the same mistake.

Here an important question arises. Is the figure of the police in Rancière not very close to what Badiou would have called a 'state'? There is a moment – in his *Ten Theses on Politics* – when Rancière hints that it does.[38] In his key text *Disagreement*, however, he clarifies that this is not the case, that the police are not equivalent to the 'state apparatus'.[39] It can be concluded that Rancière is trying to completely deontologise politics, especially at the social level. As he himself comments: 'Politics has no objects or issues of its own.'[40] This idea may remind us of Žižek's project. To put it another way, unlike Badiou, neither Rancière nor Žižek rule out the 'becoming-subject' of any factical identification whatsoever.[41] Perhaps this is why they both speak of politics in terms of a *torsion*: for them, in politics, any (social) identity whatsoever is capable of being twisted into a subjectivity (although Rancière, unlike Žižek, does not use the term torsion in a specifically dialectical sense). Rancière once alluded to the process in the following way: a 'straight line drawn by curved paths'.[42] Nevertheless, the decisive difference between Rancière and Žižek is predictable: the Marxist symptom, which Žižek possesses, of absolute social simplification – i.e. his theoretical emphasis on the proletariat as the only possible agent of emancipation – is not present in Rancière.

We believe, then, that this is what constitutes the radical nature of Rancière's intervention: he tries to avoid an ontological description, however minimal, of the social. In Rancière, there is no state (of the situation), nor is there a 'social space', nor 'the social'. We could say that Rancière radicalises Laclau's idea that 'society' is not a proper object of thought, since we do not ultimately know what it consists of. The implication of all this is that Rancière assumes that politics can happen anywhere. We understand that this is what he is referring to when he says that politics does not produce a subject *ex nihilo*.[43] Perhaps it should be emphasised here that for Rancière all this is not a question of 'generalising' politics: the heterogeneity we mentioned earlier does not imply any such thing. Remember that Rancière has argued that politics is *rare*. All he is saying is simply that the 'point of enunciation' of this politics should be considered to be radically contingent. In sum, we believe that of all the authors that we have discussed here, Rancière is the one who most clearly conceives what one could call *the absolute dispersivity of the 'social space'*. We would add that this result allows us to avoid the contradiction between antagonism in the singular and antagonisms in the plural. How so?

The key point here is that if there are different types of police, then there may be different types of politics and, even more important, if this is the case, then *it stands to reason that these types can coexist*. Furthermore, each of these forms of politics must be considered singular with respect to the specific police order from which it is separated. In conclusion, Rancière offers us a way out of the contradiction that arises from Laclau and Mouffe's theory of hegemony, stating – paradoxically (although how could we get out of this paradox?) – that antagonisms can be singular and plural at the same time. That is, an antagonism is unique with respect to a specific social situation, but more than one such situation can – and does – exist at the same time. This implies a view of political sequences that is similar to Žižek's, but now (for the first time) freed from the problem of social totalisation. It should perhaps be pointed out here that this is merely our *interpretation* of Rancière, which, as such, may be open to contestation. This is not of concern, however, since the great advantage of his work is that it has allowed us to get where we have wanted to since the beginning of this chapter. Nevertheless, we feel that, before concluding, we should deal with some potential counter-evidence. Once again, it will emerge from Laclau's criticism of Rancière.

Laclau versus Rancière

In *The Populist Reason*, Laclau comments that he feels rather akin to Rancière.[44] According to Laclau, there are two points of intersection between their projects. First, he associates 'the people' in Rancière with his own conception of it, in meta-phorical/synecdochical terms. Second, he contends that their respective conceptions of the people share the notion of ontological emptiness (to put it in Laclau's vocabulary). Next, he points out two discrepancies he has with Rancière. First, he argues that the people, understood as the 'part-that-has-no-part', could also assume a fascist orientation (all without losing its 'emptiness'). Second, although he applauds the radical emptying of the category of the people in Rancière (literally any identity or social class – so long as it is an excluded element – can become the subject of politics), he argues that Rancière betrays his own argument at a crucial point, by attributing certain 'sociological' characteristics to the proletariat, which undermines its very emptiness and, according to Laclau, has the effect of placing Rancière – like Badiou and Žižek – in a position that is essentially indistinguishable from that of classical Marxism. Are these comments fair?

If Laclau was right when he said that Rancière 'substantialises' the people by associating them with a sociological working class, it is true that it would indeed constitute a fatal flaw. However, we do not believe he is right. Badiou and Žižek make this mistake, up to a point, but Rancière does not. The key point here is that for Rancière, the proletariat must be considered merely a 'version' of the people, as we have already explained. This fact in itself would absolve him of Laclau's criticism, since it implies that this class contains a dimension (precisely the emptiness that is associated with a people) that goes beyond its socio-ontological aspect. Actually, we believe that the real difference between Laclau and Rancière is that the latter would not accept the former's argument about the metaphorical-synecdochical status of the people, since this represents a hegemonic logic. Again, we would say that this is so because Rancière takes the fundamental dispersivity of the social space much more seriously than Laclau. For the latter, a metaphorical knot is what constitutes a social order; but Rancière thinks otherwise. For the same reason, Laclau is obliged to conclude that the emancipatory or repressive (fascist) status of a people is an undecidable question at best; at worst – according to hegemony theory – the people is repressive *tout court* (an idea we shall discuss in the next chapter). Rancière, in contrast, argues that the fundamental vocation of the people is to emancipate itself, precisely due to its void status. We have always found it strange that Laclau is so proud of his conclusion that at the ontological level, it is impossible to distinguish a fascist people from a communist people.[45] To us, this idea seems perfectly disastrous.

In fact, the argument one finds in *The Populist Reason* is not Laclau's last word on Rancière. Later on, in 2012, a debate took place between the two thinkers in Buenos Aires, a debate that, we believe, introduces a topic that is much more relevant to our considerations here.[46] The heart of the debate was the question of political representation. Laclau's argument is that all politics – including populist politics – must pass through processes of representation. We already know that this is consistent with his theory of hegemony, which hypothesises an intensional (mythical) social ensemble. Theoretically speaking, this would require the condensation – that is, the representation – of some signifiers with others. In a certain sense, Rancière reaches the opposite conclusion: he argues that the people – in order to be truly considered a people – must distance itself from any representative form. He goes on to clarify that representation could perhaps be considered a legitimate form of politics, but, if this is the case, it must be considered only one of its forms, and not even the most important one, since popular politics is fundamentally presentative, rather than representative. In truth, Rancière endorses the occasional possibility of representative politics only begrudgingly, and essentially treats it as a limit case. The examples he provides come from the countries in Latin America today, and Europe in the distant past.

At this point, we must acknowledge that we are on the side of Rancière in this debate: we would fully accept his argument that politics is essentially presentative, a conclusion that is the product of our critique of the theory of hegemony. If not, we would not be dealing with singularities. On the other hand, we see a certain risk in Rancière's interpretation of his own argument. Of what order? The potential problem has to do with the temptation of – what is sometimes called – micropolitics. Does Rancière advocate this form? After all, there is a moment when he comments that politics is always a 'local' issue, and, in another, he adds that: 'There is no world politics.'[47] On the other hand, he continually discusses groups such as 'the poor', or 'proletarians'; numerically speaking, these groups are hardly small! In truth, we believe that at the theoretical level Rancière does not rule out either micropolitics or macropolitics. We have the impression that for him, the potential scope of a political struggle corresponds to that of the police from which the former is subtracted. For this reason, it is impossible to determine its extension in advance, at least conceptually, since we do not know a priori what such a police might consist of. Despite this, it is true that, at least in the early period of his work (and probably in the later one as well), one finds a certain *fascination* with local politics, which almost risks breaking with his own theoretical principles. It is very striking, for example, that in his historical works Rancière sees himself as a genealogist of what he calls 'heretical knowledge'.[48] Heresy is a rather specific political form: a rebellion that is necessarily limited in scope (since it never ultimately manages to sustain itself). At this stage of his research, Rancière treats this form almost as if its limited nature were a token of its very authenticity. Perhaps this is why he ends up associating democracy with anarchy, that is, with the absolute absence of systems of re-presentation.[49]

It should be taken into account here that the great enemy of Rancière, for almost his entire intellectual career, has been the 'political intellectuals', who, according to him, tend to distort the speech of the people, trying to translate it – always wrongly – into their own terms. In this connection, it is striking when Rancière quotes – albeit with some irony – the following poetic phrase from Rilke: 'When poor people are thinking of something one should not disturb them. Perhaps it will occur to them.'[50] It could be mentioned here that one of the first 'post-Marxist' acts of Rancière was to resuscitate the discourse of a handful of workers who were agitating in the first half of the 19th century.[51] It is almost as if the chronological distance represents the space that Rancière always intends to insert between the intellectuals and the people, or between the voice of the latter and any attempt to 'interpret' it politically. In addition, he was studying the speech of a few hundred people, that is, a tiny group. Our basic argument here is that this kind of gesture risks appearing to turn politics into something fragile and ineffable. Almost as if we were deploying a negative theology. Or even as if its tragic (that is, heretical) appearance is what defines it. Perhaps it could even be said that there is in play, here, a certain romanticisation of what Rancière calls 'the glorious proletarian body', in the very sense that its historical sequences are destined to end tragically.[52] It must be emphasised that all these points do not necessarily represent a contradiction in his theory. But on the other hand, they *appear* to be contradictory, and we believe that this can cause significant confusion. For the same reason, we would insist on the absolutely indeterminate scale of a political movement. We believe that no one should be offended if the examples of it also extend to the macropolitical! Furthermore, we think that the aforementioned problems have an important side effect, which is especially relevant to our general argument. Again, it has to do with a difference between Laclau and Rancière, this time regarding the word 'populism'.

We have seen that Laclau fully accepts the term populism, a position that we share. Rancière, on the other hand, is more resistant. Why? Once again, it's possible that the importance of this dispute should not be overstated. In the book *What Is a People?*, for example, Rancière seems to reject the term mainly for 'strategic' reasons: he sees it as tainted by media discourse.[53] In addition, it is true that at another time Rancière recognises that the pejorative use of the word – by the establishment – is an act of bad faith, which could be interpreted as an indirect defence of it.[54] On the other hand, it is clear that he does not see the term as especially useful at a political level. This aspect of his project likely reflects his problem with political representation: the moment a people seems to 'represent itself' in a populist movement, it risks being lost. We believe, however, that it is not necessary – and even that it can be harmful – to make this theoretical leap, since we consider that it may represent an a priori illegitimate limit to the scope of a truly popular movement, thus condemning it, once again, to the tragic status of a micropolitics. We even think that it may constitute a theoretical confusion about the true nature of populist leadership, but we shall have to leave this point aside for the moment (it will be taken up in the second half of the book). In sum, we think that retaining the term populism is necessary because it gives an important theoretical signal of our distance from any heretical and unproductive anarchism. Unlike Rancière, we remain faithful to this word, even if it is now in a strictly presentative mode.

Conclusion

Let's summarise all that we have said so far. In the first place, we argued that Laclau was right when he advocated the concept of a people, in part because this term allows him to avoid the problem of the political status of the contemporary proletariat. Furthermore, we applauded Laclau and Mouffe's decision to reject the thesis of the historical simplification of the social space. We celebrated the fact that this decision allows us to contemplate the diversity of struggles that exist today. However, we added that when these authors tried to combine this intuition with their theory of hegemony, its logical validity collapsed: the supposed absolute emptiness of the term 'people' was found to be overdetermined by the hegemonic processes themselves. Next, we argued that the validity of emptiness is recovered in the theory of the communist Badiou, who insists on the absolute singularity of antagonism, but we added that he too contradicts his own theory, when he imposes a 'social' limit on said antagonism. Next, we considered the work of another 'communist', Žižek, who opened up the possibility of a singular antagonism that would not be limited by any social ontology. But then we discovered that Žižek also betrays his own theory, by returning to a classically Marxist social ontology, even if the latter is based on a reinterpretation of its Hegelian foundations. Finally, we argued that Rancière cuts the Gordian knot, by insisting on the absolute singularity of each antagonism, in addition to its possible – and paradoxical – proliferation in a social realm whose extension can never finally be defined. In the same sense, we believe it is logical that Rancière also uses the term 'people' to describe the subject of political antagonism, since it is the only word that respects the ontological emptiness of the situations in which such subjects find themselves. On the other hand, we disagree with Rancière on the question of whether it is possible to use the term populism to describe the political movement that accompanies this people. We think that it is still important to deploy this term if we want to avoid the trap of a tragic micropolitics. In conclusion, we believe that *populism is the only political form that is capable of emptying out every social ontology.* Surely a doubt will arise here. What about the seemingly unifying character of a *state*, even a nation-state? Doesn't this impose on us de facto a unified social formation, which therefore almost forces us to adopt a hegemonic strategy: what has sometimes been called (to use an obvious oxymoron) 'strategic essentialism'? Here we arrive at what is perhaps our most radical conclusion.

First of all, we believe that the two component terms of the phrase 'nation-state' should be separated out. Since we believe that every political struggle is 'essentially' different, we do not believe that an antagonism with respect to the figure of the nation can be reduced to any other. The state, however, is another matter. We would concede that the dispute over the state does not have the same character as other struggles. So how should we think about it, from our revised perspective? Given all that has been argued so far, the conclusion is probably inevitable. We would argue that there is not a single state, but a series of infinite and scattered practices that is sometimes referred to – incorrectly – as a unified state. The proof of this is simply the fact that – to put it in Badiouian terms – the fundamental name of being is the void, and furthermore that there are as many voids as there are situations. Therefore, what is often called the state, understood as a social formation, is also infected with a fundamental dispersivity. Is this counter-intuitive? Maybe.

On the other hand, if one looks at the great contemporary analysts of the state, one sees that it has been extremely difficult for them to give a single theoretical form to the object of their analysis. Who are we talking about exactly? A fundamental reference in this regard is Bob Jessop, who has spent decades studying the issue. What does he have to say on it?

First of all, Jessop states that 'it is clear that the existence of "the state" cannot be judged in simple yes/no terms'.[55] This fundamental indecisiveness about his own object is notable, although it would be logical for him to try to give some kind of structure to his speculations. Hence the following, minimal definition:

> The core of the state apparatus comprises a relatively unified ensemble of socially-embedded, socially regularized, and strategically selective institutions and organizations whose socially accepted function is to define and enforce collectively binding decisions on the members of a society in a given territorial area in the name of the common interest or general will of an imagined political community identified with that territory.[56]

The many contingencies contained in this definition can be seen immediately: 'core', 'relatively unified', 'ensemble', 'socially accepted function', 'imagined political community'. But even this definition – with all its caveats – it is too strong for Jessop, who immediately adds further conditions, six in number: i) 'Above, around, and below the core of the state ensemble are institutions and organizations whose relationship with the core ensemble is uncertain'; ii) 'The nature of these institutions and organizations, their articulation to form the ensemble, and their links with the wider society all depend on the nature and history of the social formation'; iii) 'Although the socially acknowledged nature of a state's political functions for society is a defining feature of normal states, the forms in which this is institutionalized and expressed vary'; iv) 'While coercion is the state's *ultimate* sanction, a state also has other means of intervention at its disposal, both material and symbolic'; v) 'The society whose common interest and general will are administered in line with the state idea is no more an empirical given than the state is'; vi)

> Whatever the political rhetoric of the common interest or general will might suggest, these are always 'illusory' insofar as attempts at definition occur on a strategically biased structural and discursive terrain and involve the differential articulation and aggregation of interests, opinions and values.[57]

After reading all of this, one has the feeling that the 'minimal definition' of Jessop's state has begun to run through one's fingers like sand. To be fair to the author, the empirical component of his work is incredibly well developed. But the truth is that this same merit later generates another problem. The empirical complexity of his work raises the question of the usefulness of its theoretical adjunct. If every phenomenon is an exception, where is the norm? So Jessop ends up drawing conclusions like the following: 'states are not omnicompetent'[58] and 'the state has no inherent substantive unity *qua* institutional ensemble'.[59] Even when he speaks of 'state projects' – a term that refers to movements of social transformation – he comments that:

> state actions should not be ascribed to *the* state as an originating subject but should be seen as the emergent, unintended, and complex resultant of what rival 'states within the state' or competing social forces have done and are doing, on a complex strategic terrain.[60]

Jessop's ultimate conclusion is this: 'the state is polymorphous'.[61]

The most important influence on Jessop's post-Marxist approach was the Gramscian theory of Nicos Poulantzas. In his classic book *State, Power, Socialism*, Poulantzas – another lover of theoretical and empirical complexity – concludes that 'there is no general theory of the State because there can never be one'.[62] Essentially, Poulantzas treats the state as the material condensation of struggles between, and within, social classes. Hence its irreducible complexity. But what about the apparent bureaucratic and legal unity of the state, which for many is highly intuitive? Poulantzas dismisses it, saying:

> We must therefore discard once and for all the view of the State as a completely united mechanism, founded on a homogeneous and hierarchical distribution of the centres of power moving from top to bottom of a uniform ladder or pyramid. According to this conception, the homogeneity and uniformity of the exercise of power is ensured by juridical regulation within the State: by a constitutional and administrative law that demarcates the fields of competence and activity of the various apparatuses. This is a radically false image, however. Of course, the present-day State does possess a hierarchical and bureaucratic structure, and it does indeed exhibit the characteristics of centralism. But these features do not resemble their juridical representation in any way whatsoever – not in France, the land of centralizing Jacobinism in the tradition of Absolutist monarchy, and not in any other country.[63]

And the political projects to transform the state? Poulantzas concludes that:

> Rather than facing a corps of state functionaries and personnel united and cemented around a univocal political will, we are dealing with fiefs, clans and factions: a multiplicity of diversified micro-policies. However coherent each of these may appear in isolation, they are nevertheless mutually contradictory; and the policy of the State essentially consists in the outcome of their collision, rather than in the (more or less successful) application of the global objective of the state apex.[64]

It seems that what these authors are really doing is fully incorporating Trotsky's principle of combined and uneven development into their thinking. What we propose – based on our own 'ontological' principles – is that we take a further, small, theoretical step. We would argue that the empirico-theoretical complexity of the state as a unit, so clearly identified and analysed by the sophisticated authors just mentioned, is indeed an effect of its fundamental dispersivity and, ultimately, its non-existence. Is it still possible, from this perspective, to speak of the state as such? Perhaps the answer can be found in a comment by Jessop himself. He claims that many political actors end up acting towards the state 'as if' it existed. We certainly would accept the existence of an 'imaginary' state formation (to use the psychoanalytic term), probably as a result of an obscure human desire for unity and coherence. But it is only in this sense that we would concede that it is still possible to speak of the concept.

We would like to add a final point here. We believe that a politics that respects the singularity of populist antagonism, in the context of a social field understood *qua* pure dispersion – a society-without-one, so to speak – needs a theoretical name, to be able to identify itself. We propose to use the term *emancipation* to distinguish it. We believe that this word is a good substitute for 'revolution', since while the latter captures well the dimension of rupture – separation from an existing social situation – that politics necessarily possesses, on the other hand, it also implies that antagonistic politics should be understood as, in some way, a total and totalising process, which also – since it has to reduce everything to a single antagonism – has the habit of standardising all that it encounters. In this sense, emancipation captures the diversity of existing struggles. Actually, this word is used by almost all the 'post-Marxist' authors we have cited in this chapter. Perhaps Badiou has been the most direct in relation to this aspect, especially with regard to the chronology that we have mentioned. He has spoken of: 'politics – at least the politics that matter to thought, that is emancipatory politics, once called revolutionary politics'.[65] Rancière also uses the term constantly, to describe his political proposal, that of the 'verification' of the hypothesis of equality.

Laclau has been more sceptical with regard to the term *emancipation*, probably because he indeed associated it with *revolution* in the classical sense. But we have already explained why we believe that Laclau reaches this conclusion: it is difficult for him to ultimately choose between an emancipatory and a non-emancipatory politics, due to his fundamental indecisiveness regarding the singularity and plurality of antagonisms within a social field that he considers to be unified. Perhaps this is why he concedes, at a certain point, that, despite his reservations regarding the term, we should not consent to 'a simple abandonment of the logic of emancipation'.[66] In sum, for us, an emancipatory politics should from now on be considered that which militates in regard to specific antagonisms, and never attempts to subordinate some struggles to others in the name of a non-existent social state. Now that we feel we have laid out our theoretical premises, in the following chapters we should like to consider some of their general politico-theoretical implications. The latter are associated with the debates that have traditionally surrounded the issue of populism. We shall start with the classic question of whether populism should be considered a left-wing or a right-wing phenomenon.

Notes

1 For a good summary of the European sequence, see: Marina Prentoulis, *Left Populism in Europe: Lessons from Jeremy Corbyn to Podemos* (London: Pluto), 2021.
2 Ernesto Laclau, *Politics and Ideology in Marxist Ideology: Capitalism, Fascism, Populism* (London: Verso), 2011, p. 107.
3 Ernesto Laclau, *Politics and Ideology in Marxist Ideology: Capitalism, Fascism, Populism* (London: Verso), 2011, p. 196.
4 Ernesto Laclau, *New Reflections on the Revolution of Our Time* (London: Verso), 1990, pp. 60–61.
5 Ernesto Laclau, *Politics and Ideology in Marxist Ideology: Capitalism, Fascism, Populism* (London: Verso), 2011, p. 166.
6 George Wilhelm Friedrich Hegel, *Lectures on the Philosophy of World History – Introduction* (Cambridge: Cambridge University Press), 1975.
7 Chantal Mouffe, *For a Left Populism* (London: Verso), 2019, pp. 10–11.
8 Jan-Werner Müller, *What Is Populism?* (London: Penguin), 2017, pp. 2–3.
9 Cas Mudde and Cristóbal Rovira Kaltwasser, *Populism – A Very Short Introduction* (Oxford: Oxford University Press), 2017, pp. 5–6 (emphasis in the original text).
10 He speaks, for example, of: 'the specific autonomy of popular-democratic interpellations.' (Ernesto Laclau, *Politics and Ideology in Marxist Ideology: Capitalism, Fascism, Populism* (London: Verso), 2011, p. 125.)
11 Ernesto Laclau, *Politics and Ideology in Marxist Ideology: Capitalism, Fascism, Populism* (London: Verso), 2011, p. 196 (emphasis in the original text).
12 Ernesto Laclau and Chantal Mouffe, *Hegemony and Socialist Strategy – Towards a Radical Democratic Politics* (London: Verso), 1985, p. 7.
13 Leon Trotsky, *History of the Russian Revolution* (Chicago: Haymarket), p. 5.
14 See: Roman Jakobson, Two Aspects of Language and Two Types of Aphasic Disturbances, in: Roman Jakobson and Morris Halle (Eds.), *Fundamentals of Language* (The Hague: Mouton and Co.), 1956, pp. 55–83.
15 Judith Butler, Ernesto Laclau and Slavoj Žižek, *Contingency, Hegemony and Universality – Contemporary Dialogues on the Left* (London: Verso), 2000, p. 303.
16 Ernesto Laclau and Chantal Mouffe, *Hegemony and Socialist Strategy – Towards a Radical Democratic Politics* (London: Verso), 1985, p. 131.
17 Ernesto Laclau and Chantal Mouffe, *Hegemony and Socialist Strategy – Towards a Radical Democratic Politics* (London: Verso), 1985, p. 122.
18 In this section, I will summarise the fundaments of the argument that is set out in what I consider to be Alain Badiou's theoretical masterpiece, *Being and Event* (London: Continuum), 2005.
19 Alain Badiou, *Logics of Worlds: Being and Event 2* (London: Continuum), 2009.
20 Ernesto Laclau, *New Reflections on the Revolution of Our Time* (Buenos Aires: New Vision), 2000.
21 The phrase – '*principled distance*' – is Peter Hallward's. See: Peter Hallward, Editorial Introduction, *Angelaki – Journal of the Theoretical Humanities*, Vol. 8, No. 2, August 2003, p. 111.
22 Alain Badiou, *Our Wound Is Not so Recent* (London: Polity), 2016, p. 83.
23 See: Peter Hallward (Ed.), *Think Again – Alain Badiou and the Future of Philosophy* (London: Continuum), 2004, pp. 131, 137.
24 Peter Hallward (Ed.), *Think Again – Alain Badiou and the Future of Philosophy* (London: Continuum), 2004, pp. 134–135.
25 Alain Badiou, *San Pablo – The Foundation of Universalism* (Barcelona: Anthropos), 1999, p. 11.
26 Slavoj Žižek, Beyond Discourse Analysis, in: Ernesto Laclau (Ed.), *New Reflections on the Revolution of Our Time* (London: Verso), 1990, pp. 249–260.

27 Slavoj Žižek, *The Sublime Object of Ideology* (London: Verso), 1989, p. 5.

28 Slavoj Žižek, *The Parallax View* (Cambridge, MA: MIT), 2009, p. 55.

29 Slavoj Žižek, *Did Somebody Say Totalitarianism? – Five Interventions in the (Mis)Use of a Notion* (London: Verso), 2001, p. 140.

30 Ernesto Laclau, *On Populist Reason* (London: Verso), 2005, p. 237.

31 www.lacan.com/ziztrap.htm; Slavoj Žižek, *The Ticklish Subject: The Absent Center of Political Ontology* (London: Verso), 1999, pp. 134–135; www.salon.com/2015/10/11/slavoj_zizek_on_obama_bernie_sex_and_democracy_thats_the_reality_of_global_capitalism_everyone_is_violating_the_rules/.

32 The following summary is based on the argument of Jacques Rancière, *Dis-Agreement – Politics and Philosophy* (Minneapolis, MN: University of Minnesota Press), 1999.

33 Jacques Rancière, *Staging the People* (London: Verso), 2019, p. 15.

34 Jacques Rancière, *Dis-Agreement – Politics and Philosophy* (Minneapolis, MN: University of Minnesota Press), 1999, p. 32.

35 Jacques Rancière, *Dis-Agreement – Politics and Philosophy* (Minneapolis, MN: University of Minnesota Press), 1999, p. 89.

36 Jacques Rancière, *Dis-Agreement – Politics and Philosophy* (Minneapolis, MN: University of Minnesota Press), 1999, p. 59.

37 Jacques Rancière, *Dis-Agreement – Politics and Philosophy* (Minneapolis, MN: University of Minnesota Press), 1999, p. 50.

38 Jacques Rancière, Ten Theses on Politics, in: *Dissensus – On Politics and Aesthetics* (London: Continuum), 2010.

39 Jacques Rancière, *Dis-Agreement – Politics and Philosophy* (Minneapolis, MN: University of Minnesota Press), 1999, p. 29.

40 Jacques Rancière, *Dis-Agreement – Politics and Philosophy* (Minneapolis, MN: University of Minnesota Press), 1999, p. 31.

41 Jacques Rancière, *Dis-Agreement – Politics and Philosophy* (Minneapolis, MN: University of Minnesota Press), 1999, p. 36.

42 Jacques Rancière, *Proletarian Nights: The Workers' Dream in Nineteenth-Century France* (London: Verso), 2010, p. 134.

43 Jacques Rancière, *Dis-Agreement – Politics and Philosophy* (Minneapolis, MN: University of Minnesota Press), 1999, p. 36.

44 Ernesto Laclau, *On Populist Reason* (London: Verso), 2005, p. 245.

45 Ernesto Laclau, *On Populist Reason* (London: Verso), 2005, p. 246.

46 www.versobooks.com/blogs/2008-don-t-they-represent-us-a-discussion-between-jacques-ranciere-and-ernesto-laclau.

47 Jacques Rancière, *Dis-Agreement – Politics and Philosophy* (Minneapolis, MN: University of Minnesota Press), 1999, p. 139.

48 Jacques Rancière, *Staging the People* (London: Verso), 2019, p. 34.

49 https://autonomies.org/2017/05/jacques-ranciere-the-anarchy-of-democracy/.

50 Jacques Rancière, *Staging the People* (London: Verso), 2019, p. 32.

51 Jacques Rancière, *Proletarian Nights: The Workers' Dream in Nineteenth-Century France* (London: Verso), 2012.

52 Jacques Rancière, *Staging the People* (London: Verso), 2019, p. 8.

53 Alain Badiou, Pierre Bourdieu, Judith Butler, Georges Didi Huberman, Sadri Khiari and Jacques Rancière, *What Is a People?* (New York: Columbia University Press), 2013.

54 Jacques Rancière, *Staging the People* (London: Verso), 2019, p. 19.

55 Bob Jessop, *The State: Past, Present, Future* (Cambridge: Polity), 2016, p. 45.

56 Bob Jessop, *The State: Past, Present, Future* (Cambridge: Polity), 2016, p. 49.

57 Bob Jessop, *The State: Past, Present, Future* (Cambridge: Polity), 2016, pp. 50–51.

58 Bob Jessop, *The State: Past, Present, Future* (Cambridge: Polity), 2016, p. 70.

59 Bob Jessop, *The State: Past, Present, Future* (Cambridge: Polity), 2016, p. 85.

60 Bob Jessop, *The State: Past, Present, Future* (Cambridge: Polity), 2016, p. 86 (emphasis in the original).
61 Bob Jessop, *The State: Past, Present, Future* (Cambridge: Polity), 2016, p. 111.
62 Nicos Poulantzas, *State, Power, Socialism* (London: Verso), 2014, p. 20.
63 Nicos Poulantzas, *State, Power, Socialism* (London: Verso), 2014, pp. 133–134.
64 Nicos Poulantzas, *State, Power, Socialism* (London: Verso), 2014, pp. 135–136.
65 Alain Badiou, *Conditions* (London: Bloomsbury), 2017, p. 147.
66 Ernesto Laclau, *Emancipation(s)* (London: Verso), 1996, p. 2.

Part II

Chapter 2

Is populism left-wing or right-wing?

Let's take a moment to contemplate the tragic situation in which Cas Mudde, the Dutch political scientist, finds himself. Mudde is considered the world's leading expert on populism. Whenever a major magazine, or publisher, wants to issue something on the subject, Mudde is the first person they call. For example, he was the lead author in the Oxford University Press book *Populism: A Very Short Introduction*.[1] However, in those moments when Mudde is asked to give his personal opinion on his signature subject, he opines that it should be abandoned as a political horizon. In fact, he takes this position because he is on the left (and perhaps also – one could speculate – because he comes from northern Europe), and he considers that what the left should really do is return to its social-democratic roots, thus undermining the new populism that he himself has analysed so successfully. It might be added that Mudde is not only an expert on populism but also on the extreme right (his brother was a relatively famous Dutch far-right activist) and he fundamentally seems to associate populism with the latter. This attitude is expressed, for example, in the long essay on populism that he wrote in 2019 for *The Guardian*, in which he describes the topic as an almost exclusively right-wing phenomenon.[2] For most of the article, he practically makes the term 'right-wing populism' into a syntagm. When the time comes for him to talk about left-wing populism, in the dying moments of the essay, he does so briefly and almost contemptuously.

It should be recognised that Mudde's position is quite common in much of 'civilised' society, which sees populism as vulgar, regressive and inauthentic. We see things a little differently. Nevertheless, given the contempt that many people have for the term and given also the near-automatic association for many people between populism and the extreme right (above all in the academy), perhaps it would be a good idea to provide an explanation for the discrepancy. After all, it is a confusion that can easily arise, especially when you see a person like Nigel Farage invoking 'real people' to justify whatever political hobby horse he has decided to jump on that week. In this chapter, then, we will try to answer the question of whether populism should be considered right-wing or left-wing. Logically, three possible positions present themselves: i) populism can be either right-wing or left-wing; ii) populism is right-wing; iii) populism is left-wing. We will examine them

DOI: 10.4324/9781003431916-5

one by one, and thus we will see which fits best with the premises that we outlined in the previous chapter.

Populism can be either right-wing or left-wing

The idea that populism can be either right-wing or left-wing is defended by Laclau and Mouffe, among others. This means that it is consistent with their theory of hegemony. How so? First, it must be remembered that these two authors believe that all politics have the same structure. This is reflected, for example, in the specific interpretation that Laclau makes of Heidegger's ontological difference. Laclau believes that on the one hand we have abstract ontological categories, and on the other, their corresponding ontical contents. This interpretation of the Heideggerian distinction is probably debatable. It tends to ignore, for example, the radical – and therefore disruptive – character of ontological difference itself. However, this is not the most important issue here. The key point is that according to Laclau and Mouffe, nothing specific about the ontic (regional) content of a political movement can be deduced from its ontological (general) form. What does this form consist of? We explained it earlier on: there is a field, delimited by an antagonism, now understood as the flip-side of a hegemonic signifier, which supposedly condenses a further series of antagonisms. It is true that in this schema, the question of being on the right or on the left does not arise. Does this imply that for the above authors it is not necessary to distinguish right-wing hegemony from left-wing hegemony, because they are essentially the same thing? Not quite. They believe that the formal structure of politics dictates that both are possible, but they do not deduce from this that they are entirely indistinguishable. So, how do they propose to separate the two?

The criterion introduced by Laclau and Mouffe derives from their reading of Gramsci. Chantal Mouffe mentions it in her recent book on populism, but in reality it is something that has been present in all the Gramscian authors who have worked in the same field as Laclau and Mouffe, especially in England: in the pages, for example, of the revisionist magazine of the British Communist Party, *Marxism Today*. What I have in mind here is the Gramscian principle of 'transformism' (or 'passive revolution'). Transformism describes the moment when an 'organic crisis' (to use Gramsci's own term) in a social system is resolved in a conservative rather than a 'progressive' direction. How are these two results distinguished? A transformist resolution of a social crisis would be when said system manages to consolidate itself. A progressive solution is when the previous system is, generally speaking, replaced by another: essentially, in Gramsci's traditionally Marxist vision, one in which the ruling class is the proletariat. As we commented before, Laclau and Mouffe would not accept this last characteristic: they do not believe in the historical pre-eminence of the proletariat. On the other hand, they do accept the idea that when the plurality of demands that supposedly float freely in a society during an organic crisis are once again incorporated into the existing majority (the previous hegemony), we are faced with a transformist logic, and when these demands produce a generally new social configuration, then we are witnessing a 'progressive' change. The word *progressive* might cause confusion here. One thinks of Lacan's phrase: 'there is no progress. What we gain on one side we lose on the other. Since we don't know what we've lost, we think we've won'. The fundamental problem here is that 'progress' seems to imply a view of history as a total process, which takes us closer to the Marxist concept of the necessary laws of history, a concept with which Laclau and Mouffe would not concur. Despite the fact that they reject this idea, however, they do seem to accept that there can be a net consolidation or a net reorganisation of a social system. In the first case, they would say that we are dealing with a right-wing hegemony and in the second with a left-wing hegemony. Moreover, since they believe that hegemony goes hand in hand with populism, one can see how they end up concluding that it is possible for populism to be either left- or right-wing.

An important factor in these formulations seems to be that of *time*. That is to say, sometimes populism will attempt to introduce new forms of social organisation, and sometimes it endeavours to return to the past. From this perspective, 'the people' can be understood either as a people to come, or as a people that has been lost. This argument has further theoretical implications. For example, it could be said that the future represents an open or uncertain horizon, while the past is a closed and fixed reference. Another way of understanding the same distinction is to say that a politics that focuses on the future is universalistic, while one that focuses on the past is particularistic. Thus, a past people is exclusive, whilst a people of the future can be said to be inclusive. This would echo another binary that comes from the work of Mudde and Kaltwasser: 'exclusionary' versus 'inclusionary' populism.[3] This distinction can be easily grasped if one compares, for example, fascist (right-wing) propaganda with that of the (left-wing) communists. Fascism offers a political project from the past, for the few, and communism a project for the future, for all. If one thinks about the history of what is called populism, one notices that it has traditionally been made up of both emancipatory ideas – by definition, futural ones – and regressive ideas. The original populists in the U.S. wanted to break up the banks (an unprecedented demand), but they also wanted to remove the entire railway network from the country (which would have meant going back to an earlier historical stage). Laclau and Mouffe would probably regard this as an example of politically mixed populism. In conclusion, for these authors, all the cases mentioned previously would be examples of hegemony; the temporal aspect simply decides whether or not they can be considered politically reactionary or not. Is this idea coherent?

It is clear that this argument is based on the premise that several different demands (antagonisms) exist in a social formation. Hence the idea of using two different epithets: transformist or progressive. We have already explained our problem with this premise: to us, it seems self-contradictory. So, if what we have argued is true – that strictly speaking, only one antagonism can exist in a social formation – we would automatically lose Laclau and Mouffe's criterion for distinguishing between right-wing and left-wing populism. Now, if our position is that each antagonism is singular and also *irruptive* (as we argued in the first chapter of this book), can we conclude that all populism is left-wing, even basing ourselves – to some extent – on the premises of Laclau and Mouffe? Not so fast.

First of all, Laclau and Mouffe's conception, according to which we could add or subtract elements, would imply that we have an idea of the extension of the space in which such a manoeuvre could occur. As was explained in the previous chapter, this is in fact the corollary of any theory based on the uniqueness of a social space. On the other hand, there are theories of this type – those of Badiou and Žižek, for example – that, despite maintaining said uniqueness, continue to insist on the divided character of the relevant space. To be clear, at an abstract level Laclau and Mouffe would insist on the same. But then they make a second move, which complicates the picture. The very Gramscian distinction that they introduce, between transformist and progressive forces, is actually based on the idea of a 'seizure of power', within a unique space, in the name of one or the other such force. Literally, it is a hegemonic moment. If this were not the case, the aforementioned distinction would not make sense. At the very moment of taking power, however, the *void* of this space would automatically be filled, and the moment of political antagonism as such would disappear. Moreover, since the moment of repressing the void is, in fact, the essence of transformism, we must conclude that, according to Laclau and Mouffe's own criteria, all hegemonic politics is transformist. In other words, the indecision between plural and singular antagonisms in the work of Laclau and Mouffe, which we have previously discussed, is here converted into a form of politico-theoretical conservatism. This in fact takes us to our second proposition: that populism should be considered right-wing. We think it would be interesting, at this point, to explore how Badiou – that great advocate of the singularity of an antagonism – treats this issue.

Populism is right-wing

We have already explained that Badiou specifies that what he calls a subject is an agent that adheres to the void of a situation. That is why he argues that an 'evental site' may be found 'on the edge of the void'.[4] This is how he defines singularity, an idea that we also consider to be the basis of the 'people', in populism. On the other hand, Badiou adds – in his book *Ethics* – that if a political subject, after being born (because before the event, this subject does not exist), adheres to the *plenitude* of said situation, then instead of being empty, we are in fact faced with one of the main ways of abandoning, or suffocating, the event with which it is associated. This is not a straightforward process, because once it has been subtracted from a situation, an event cannot simply be ignored; it has to be violently renounced. Under these circumstances, something that looks like an event occurs but is actually what Badiou calls a *simulacrum* of it. The paradigm of the simulacrum, for Badiou, is Nazism. This is so because Badiou considers it a bad copy of his favourite example of the event: the Russian Revolution. To put it succinctly, a simulacrum has all the violence – or more – of an event, but none of the emancipation. This last idea reminds us of the German philosopher Walter Benjamin's apocryphal comment, that every fascist emergence testifies to a failed revolution.[5] It can even be seen as a variation of Marx's idea that history happens twice: first as tragedy and second as farce. It also explains why the frequent liberal assimilation of fascism to communism (and vice versa) is so misleading. Both can be very violent, in the sense that they involve a break with an existing situation, but their ultimate aims are completely different. One wants the world to change, while the other wants it to stop changing. That is why one of them – fascism – is based on excluding a specific group from the social totality, while the other fights – sometimes violently – to include everyone. It is true that the superficial effects of these two processes can seem to be very similar: from the point of view of a victim of political violence, it may not matter very much to you whether the person who is attacking you is on the left or the right. Still, the theoretical distinction must be retained if we want to avoid total confusion.

If Badiou's argument is accepted, then the challenge for the theory of hegemony is obvious. Hegemony is based on the search for plenitude precisely because it theorises a 'taking of power' within an intensional social set, after constituting itself through an antagonism. Thus, it resembles Badiou's simulacrum: by definition it is a subject that wants to return to the past, in the sense of reinforcing the plenitude of a social situation. After all, what is transformism if it is not this? From this perspective, it is impossible to imagine – at least at the theoretical level – a 'hegemonic bloc' that is not right-wing. Furthermore, if hegemony is understood as a synonym of populism, it could now be concluded that populism is necessarily right-wing. Actually, this would be an example of what in political science has traditionally been called *corporatism*, according to which the social order is seen as a replete body. It could be added that this figure has often been associated with fascism. Perhaps it is now easier to understand why so many people automatically associate populism with the right.

Are we being fair to Laclau and Mouffe here? After all, they are famously left-wing thinkers. To put it another way, they are 'progressives'. However, a person's political views are one thing; the structure and implications of their theory are another entirely. The two do not necessarily coincide. Let's look at another example of the problem, this time from Laclau's 1990 essay, *New Reflections on the Revolution of Our Time*. In this text, Laclau introduces the category of the subject for the first time, partly under the influence of Žižek. As we have explained, Laclau – like Žižek – sees this subject as a lack (a void, to put it in Badiou's more philosophical language). Next, he argues that the main political production of a subject, understood in this way, is what he calls a *myth*. It could even be said that there is a parallel between this concept and that of the subjective production of an event in Badiou (which the latter calls an *evental sequence*): a myth is something that is subtracted from a sedimented social situation. That is, just like a subject, a myth is on the side of the inaugural. Later, however, Laclau gives a curious twist to this position; he argues that an exceptionally successful myth will become an *imaginary*. What does this mean?

The term 'imaginary' is psychoanalytic. In (Lacanian) psychoanalysis, the imaginary is the realm of the *ego*. It is defined, essentially, by the urge for *unification*, or – once again – plenitude, which Lacan sees precisely as the prerogative of the *ego*. It arises from that phase of child development that he calls 'the mirror stage', in which an infant first identifies with the apparently unified image he sees when he looks in the mirror.[6] Lacan himself provided an interpretation of the social effects of the *ego*, in an early article on what he calls the 'family complexes'; In a subsection of this text called '*The Nostalgia for Wholeness*', he comments:

> The saturation of the complex is the foundation of maternal feelings; its sublimation contributes to family sentiments; its liquidation leaves traces in which it can be detected since it is this structure of the imago that remains at the base of the mental processes that have remodelled it. If we had to define the most abstract form in which it is found, we would characterize it as a perfect assimilation of totality to being. In this formula, a bit philosophical in appearance, will be recognised the nostalgias of humanity: the metaphysical mirage of universal harmony; the mystical abyss of affective fusion; the social utopia of totalitarian dependency – all derived from the longings for a paradise lost before birth and from the most obscure aspirations for death.[7]

In short, the imaginary is nothing more than a – pathological – figure of unification. So if, as Laclau argues, the moment of hegemony implies the installation of a social imaginary, its only possibility is that of unifying a social field. In such an act, the moment of emptiness is completely lost; to put it psychoanalytically, such a moment *is repressed*.

It can therefore be concluded that in the logical transition between myth and imaginary in Laclau, something falls out of the picture. You cannot go from void to plenitude without there being a remainder. This explains why Badiou, for example, sees social imaginaries as the enemy of politics, while Laclau sees them as its ally.[8] Perhaps Laclau was aware of this problem when, in his later work, he began to call the signifier of social plenitude the 'empty signifier', as if there were a direct connection between plenitude and void (although all this really demonstrates, once again, is his indecision regarding the relationship between the two). We feel that we should insist, however, on the clear difference between the two aspects. All of which underscores the previous conclusion: the desire for hegemony is ultimately a conservative desire. We might add that Žižek has come to the same conclusion. In his article 'Against the Populist Temptation', he argues that populism is by definition a kind of 'ideological mystification', since it necessarily displaces a division that is 'immanent' to the social order (represented, according to him, by the proletariat) onto the 'transcendence' of an absolutely external enemy.[9] In other words, for Žižek, it is practically impossible for populism not to end up expressing itself as racism – or social segregation – due to its structural form. How, then, might we get back to the third position we outlined earlier: that populism is necessarily left-wing? Jorge Alemán is the emblematic representative of this idea. What is his argument?

Populism is left-wing

To understand Aleman's position, it is first necessary to consider his theory of *capitalist discourse*. This is another concept that comes from Lacan, who mentioned it in an obscure colloquium in 1972.[10] Fortunately, Jorge Alemán has, in his own work, developed an intuition that Lacan expounded only briefly into an entire theory.[11] In Lacan, capitalist discourse is a variation on the four discourses that he introduces in his Seminar 17. These discourses represent social-psychological structures; in Lacan's words, they are types of social bond. The four discourses are: *the discourse of the master, the discourse of the university, the discourse of the hysteric* and *the discourse of the analyst*. Within each discourse, Lacan includes four distinct structural positions: *agent, other, product, truth.*

Each discourse contains four elements: the master signifier (S_1), knowledge (S_2), the *object a* and the divided subject ($\$$). These four elements rotate between the structural positions that we see in the diagram to form the four different discourses mentioned earlier. Another conditioning factor is that the structural elements or positions are related to each other, up to a certain point (as shown by the arrows in the diagrams of the discourses).

Capitalist discourse, however, is different from these because it does not fit into the system of rotating elements identified by Lacan. Essentially, Lacan believes that capitalist discourse is a variation – a mutation – of one of the four discourses: that of the master. If one compares the master's discourse (above) with capitalist discourse, one sees that in the latter, the positions of the master signifier, which is the agent of the discourse of the master, and the divided subject, which is in the position of truth, are inverted.

This affects the kind of agency we find in the relevant discourse: the agent now becomes the divided subject (of the unconscious), which uninterruptedly expresses itself; the truth of this discourse, which the divided subject now represses, is the master signifier, which is the signifier of order. This inversion also affects the relationships between the elements of the discourse. In the other discourses, not all the elements are related: there is never a connection between product and truth,

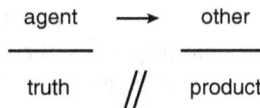

agent   ⟶   other
_____   _____
truth   **//**   product

Figure 2.1 Positions in the four discourses of Lacan.

Discourse of the master	Discourse of the university

Discourse of the hysteric	Discourse of the analyst

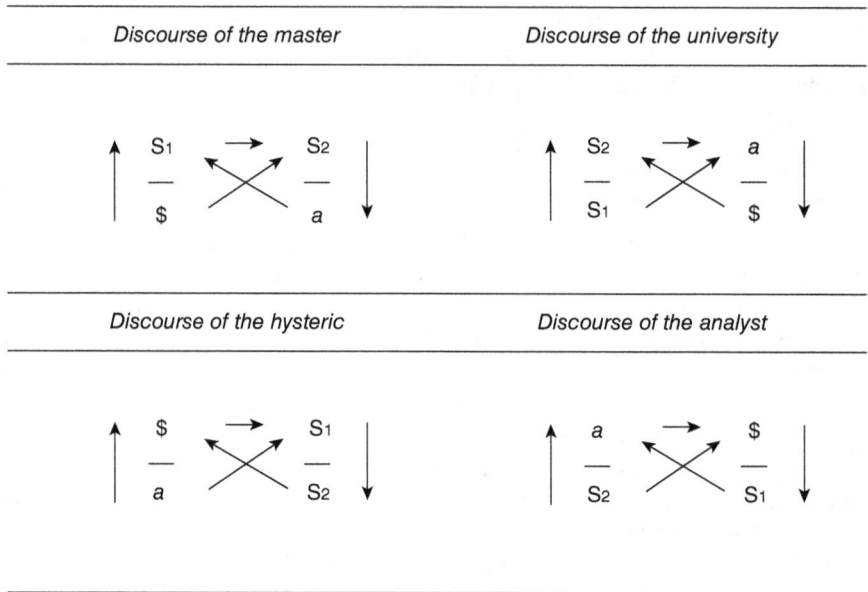

Figure 2.2 Lacan's four discourses.

Figure 2.3 Capitalist discourse.

since truth must always be understood as a discrete factor. In capitalist discourse, however, the separation between product and truth is ignored. Thus, in capitalist discourse a circuit of relations is installed (which can again be seen in the direction of the relevant arrows) between some of its elements that thereby become inseparable. In other words, it is a movement through a repetitive loop. The subject that conforms to the logic of capitalist discourse is trapped in this circuit, with no possible way out.

Jorge Alemán has applied this Lacanian theorem to the most recent phase of capitalism, which he calls neoliberal. In this situation, the subject pursues all kinds of idiotic, repetitive and vulgar *jouissance,* so as not to have to recognise at any point the demand of the master: that of parents, the authorities, etc. One implication of this argument is that in the neoliberal phase of capitalism, there can be no hegemonic logic at play, since hegemony depends – as we have explained – on the installation of a master signifier: on a principle of order, or authority (and also the presence of an enemy). This implies that in spite of the seemingly infinite extension of capitalist discourse today, the latter does not require any exercise of domination in order to establish itself. In this sense, 'neoliberalism' does not have an Other; it does not have an exterior as such. Neither is political power *stricto sensu* present in this discourse. Despite these radical conclusions, Alemán continues to defend hegemony, but now as the route to breaking away from capitalist discourse. In this sense, it is necessarily connected with the *left*, which shares this task. Can there not be a right-wing hegemony against capitalism? In his recent work, Alemán dismisses this possibility, arguing that today, the most hierarchical ('hegemonic') and therefore conservative form of right-wing politics in fact has only one task: to restore capitalist discourse as such.[12] Finally, it should be noted that Alemán associates – and this reflects the influence of Laclau and Mouffe on his work – hegemony, understood in the way we have just laid out, with populism. *Ipso facto*, for him populism is necessarily left-wing.

An interesting aspect of Alemán's conclusions is that they connect the contemporary left with *order*, which, of course, is precisely the hegemonic logic. This idea has recently become more popular on the left: capitalism is chaos, and we have to break with it by installing some sort of order. One thinks of Iñigo Errejon's recent quote: 'the greatest change that we can hope for is that of order'.[13] For our part, we do not believe it is necessary to go so far. Again, this idea is based on the moment of filling the void of a social order, something that – as we hope we have already clarified – we see as politically regressive by definition. Nevertheless, we believe that Alemán's argument is not reducible to this point. What we consider important about his position is precisely his insistence on the idea that a populist movement must be considered left-wing because it touches the singular void point of a social situation. In fact, Alemán's project contains a conceptual element that we consider perfectly describes the political productivity of an experience of the void in this sense. We have in mind his concept of *Common: Solitude* (*Soledad: Común*), which for us captures very well the dimensions of singularity (*Soledad*) and universality (*Común*) that any genuinely left-wing politics must possess.[14] We believe that this concept becomes over-complicated when Alemán assimilates it – albeit indirectly – with hegemony. With this caveat, we declare ourselves in agreement with his conclusion that populism must be considered essentially a left-wing phenomenon.[15]

However, something must be added here. When liberal European journalists talk populism down, assimilating it to the racist right, this is not, as Wittgenstein would have said, 'a stupid prejudice'.[16] It is true that racist populism has a certain connection with true populism, which comes from the left. What the two have in common is that they are both based on a real ontological difference: an antagonism. On the other hand, as we have seen, they represent two very different ways of dealing with this difference. The right tries to violently shut it down, while the left tries to make it even more visible, with the purpose of creating something new, which involves a different type of violence. Following the same logic, we believe that although populism as such is left-wing, it should be added that true populism can be perverted, thus producing a secondary and false version of it. In this sense, we propose, following Badiou, to call right-wing populism a *simulacrum* of populism. Again, a key aspect of this phenomenon is chronology. Recently, we have seen numerous examples: *Vox* occupying the space that *Podemos* opened (and then abandoned?)

in Spain, Trump walking through a political door that had already been opened by Bernie Sanders in the U.S., Bolsonaro replacing Lula and Rousseff in Brazil (although this situation has now been – albeit perhaps temporarily – reversed). One could even add the way in which the British right colonised the demand to leave the European Union, which was once proposed by the British left.

There is a deduction that can be made from this last conclusion that is probably even more controversial. It means that we must risk the simulacrum of emancipation if we want to experience emancipation in the first place. That is to say, the radical right is sometimes the price that is paid, a posteriori, for having militated in favour of a radical left. Many will see this idea as dangerous, but we think they are wrong. After all, what genuinely democratic process is risk-free? Also, what would be the alternative? To make do with what already exists? This is not an alternative that we could consent to. Badiou, in his admirably synthetic style, once expressed this idea in the following way: '*Mieux vaut un desastre qu'un désêtre*' (Better a disaster than non-being). It seems to us a pertinent comment. Perhaps part of the problem here is that popular enthusiasm is scary and many people – even some leftists – want to limit it. What can our rejection of hegemonic logic contribute on the issue of enthusiasm? We will answer in the next chapter. Once again, Laclau's treatment of the topic will be our starting point.

Notes

1 Cas Mudde and Cristóbal Rovira Kaltwasser, *Populism: A Very Short Introduction* (Oxford: Oxford University Press), 2017.
2 www.theguardian.com/news/2019/may/14/why-copying-the-populist-right-isnt-going-to-save-the-left.
3 Cas Mudde and Cristóbal Rovira Kaltwasser, Exclusionary vs. Inclusionary Populism: Comparing Contemporary Europe and Latin America, *Government and Opposition*, Vol. 48, No. 2, April 2013, pp. 147–174.
4 Alain Badiou, *Being and Event* (London: Continuum), 2005, p. 202.
5 Cited, for example, in Žižek, e.g.: www.lacan.com/essays/?page_id=261.
6 Jacques Lacan, *Écrits* (New York: Norton), 2006, pp. 75–81.
7 Jacques Lacan, *Family Complexes in the Formation of the Individual* (Chippenham: Rowe), 1994, p. 13.
8 For example, every time Badiou speaks of the imaginary in *Being and Event*, he does so pejoratively.
9 www.lacan.com/zizpopulism.htm.
10 www.elsigma.com/historia-viva/traduccion-de-la-conferencia-de-lacan-en-milan-del-12-de-mayo-de-1972/9506.
11 Especially in the book he wrote with Sergio Larriera, *Lacan: Heidegger* (Buenos Aires: Ediciones del Cipher), 1996.
12 Jorge Alemán, *Pandemónium: Notas sobre un desastre* (Madrid: NED Ediciones), 2020, pp. 43–47.
13 www.publico.es/politica/inigo-errejon-important-reform-introduce-order.html.
14 Jorge Alemán, *Soledad: Común – Políticas en Lacan* (Madrid: Clave Intelectual), 2012.
15 I have discussed this question elsewhere; see: Timothy Appleton, ¿Hay una 'diferencia ontológica' entre hegemonía populista y Soledad: Común?, in: Timothy Appleton and José Alberto Raymondi (Eds.), *Lacan en las lógicas de la emancipación – En torno a textos de Jorge Alemán* (Malaga: Miguel Gomez Ediciones), 2018, pp. 127–137.
16 Ludwig Wittgenstein, *Philosophical Investigations* (Oxford: Blackwell), 1999, p. 109.

Chapter 3

What is the connection between populism and affect?

The idea that the masses – the people – are ruled by their passions and not by reason is a traditional trope in liberal–conservative discourse. And it is still widely applied. A recent example would be the comments of the writer Simon Jenkins (on David Hume), in the house magazine of Britain's liberal classes, *Prospect*. Says Jenkins: 'Passion allowed free rein is not democracy . . . now is one of those moments when rational discourse in politics seems peculiarly vulnerable, and tribal prejudice and blind idiocy rampant'.[1] Another – this time more 'popular' – example might be the 2005 version of *War of the Worlds*, by the arch-liberal Steven Spielberg. In Spielberg's version of the story, when the Martians invade and the 'rational' state collapses, people become agitated and unstable, and engage in every kind of blind *jouissance*: killing each other or trying to get some kind of minimal advantage for themselves and their families above all others. Such examples demonstrate that popular passions are a constant phantasy of liberal culture. One even wonders if the spate of zombie movies and series in recent years is a product of this phantasy. From our perspective, however, these passions are the *sine qua non* of a populist (left) politics, and therefore they should not scare us. What are we talking about when we talk about passions, or enthusiasm? Laclau calls them 'affect'. What does he have in mind? In this chapter, we will quote him directly, on many occasions, since we find his explanations of the subject to be quite clear and concise.

Affect with hegemony

Laclau associates affect with psychoanalysis, although in reality, the great psychoanalytic influence on his work – Jacques Lacan – rejected this term, calling it – with characteristic humour – 'affective smoochy-woochy'.[2] In this sense, Laclau, not for the first time, can be said to have adopted a more Freudian position, since Freud used the term more freely. This is perhaps why Laclau sometimes associates affect with what in the Freudian tradition is called *libido*. Lacan, for his part, reinterpreted this last concept, calling it *jouissance* (enjoyment), and it is also clear that on many occasions, Laclau has this Lacanian category in mind when he speaks of the mechanisms of affect.[3] What does Laclau do with all these elements? One should recall that the basis of Laclau's theory is structuralism. This means, as we

DOI: 10.4324/9781003431916-6

explained in the first chapter, that he understands the processes of signification – including political signification – in terms of a game between metaphor and metonymy. What role does affect play in such processes? There are times when Laclau seems to see it simply in terms of a 'psychological force' that mobilises the aforementioned linguistic processes. For example, he says that:

> what rhetoric can explain is the *form* that an overdetermining investment takes, but not the *force* that explains the investment as such and its perdurability. Here something else has to be brought into the picture. Any overdetermination requires not only metaphorical condensations but also cathetic investments. That is, something belonging to the order of *affect* has a primary role in discursively constructing the social. Freud already knew it: the social link is a libidinal link.[4]

Put another way, Laclau thinks it is crucial to separate affect and signification so that they can then be linked together even more strongly: a paradoxical conclusion.

This paradox gives rise to the curious game that takes place in the book *Laclau – A Critical Reader*. In this text, Laclau and two psychoanalytic authors, Jason Glynos and Yannis Stavrakakis, compete to see who can separate affect and signification the most, only in order subsequently to show the complete immanence of the two elements. The conclusions that Laclau draws from this game are the following: 'affect . . . is not something that *is added* to signification, but something consubstantial with it'; and: 'there is no signification without affect; but, at the same time, there is no affect which is not constituted through its operation within a signifying chain'; finally: 'the dimension of affect is not something to be added to a process of signification, but something without which signification, in the first place, would not take place'.[5] We can conclude that for Laclau, the paths of affect and those of signification are essentially inseparable. Part of the problem with this conclusion is that it appears to banalise the category of affect, by making it practically ubiquitous. It should be obvious that this undermines its potential productivity, both conceptually and politically. But there are also moments in Laclau's project in which he offers us a more specific idea of the relationship between affect and signification. In what sense?

At one point, Laclau speaks of the importance to politics of what he calls *radical investment*. He adds: 'some of the categories that I employ, such as "radical investment", would be unintelligible without the notion of *jouissance*'.[6] In other words, he sees radical investment as constituting the affective dimension of politics. The word 'radical', in this context, emphasises the contingent character of such a process.[7] Here one begins to glimpse a fundamental connection between affect and pure contingency, which we shall come back to later on. Moreover, the moment of radical investment must be considered highly important, but at the same time utterly inaccessible. Laclau's word is 'impossible'. This last idea – which is also derived from Lacan, who sees the passage to the impossible as a key moment for the subject of the clinic, to the point of assimilating it to the psychoanalytic cure – does not imply that this moment never occurs, but rather that it is presented as impossible until the moment in which it is finally realised. This also means that its implications can only be grasped retroactively (which is another Lacanian–Hegelian principle). This theory also gives an idea of how 'miraculous' – also in the sense of absolutely unexpected – politics can seem, even though Laclau stayed away from that particular word. Again, we will come back to it later on. One descriptor that Laclau does use to describe this kind of experience is *ethical*.[8] He comments: 'Only if I live an action as incarnating an impossible fullness transcending it does the investment become an *ethical* investment'.[9] In other words, the ethical, for Laclau, consists in committing – affectively – to the – apparently impossible – processes of social change. Another important aspect of *jouissance* in Lacan's psychoanalytic project is that it has an object (or rather, it is not without an object).[10] For Lacan, the object of *jouissance* is the *object a* (in one of its key dimensions). We discussed Žižek's use of this term in the first chapter: we are dealing with a void object that corresponds to the void subject. From a certain point on, Laclau uses it as well. He asserts, for example, that: 'there is no achievable *jouissance* except through radical investment in an *objet petit a*.'[11]

All of these innovations reflect what could be called a 'psychoanalytic turn' in Laclau's work, which occurs after 1990. As we have discussed before, what triggered this shift was the influence that Slavoj Žižek had on his work. It all started with the incorporation into Laclau's project of the Lacanian theory of the subject that Žižek had already promoted. Indeed, if an essential component of the subject of psychoanalysis is affect, or *jouissance*, it is not surprising that Laclau, following the incorporation of such a subject into his theoretical discourse, ended up analysing this aspect. Moreover, this dimension entailed other concepts. From that moment on, Laclau brought in the concept of *the universal*, which represented a nuancing of his earlier concept of the equivalential; he also introduced the previously mentioned concept of the *empty signifier*, which can be considered a development of his concept of the floating signifier; and he introduced the concept of *dislocation*, which was a revised version of his concept of antagonism.[12] What kind of variation was in play, in each of these cases? It seems to us that in these examples, a dimension of *process* was opened up. Dislocation describes a moment in which antagonism is experienced, the empty signifier is the moment in which a floating signifier is extended to the point where it shows the limits of a system of signification, and the universal represents the moment in which the equivalential is charged with an element of non-being. Again, all these processes depend on the inclusion of a dimension of affect (or *jouissance*): a 'radical investment'. In sum, the specificity and providence of the category of affect, in Laclau's work, is the fact that it necessarily accompanies temporal processes, through which, one assumes, social change will be carried out. Here one glimpses a connection with the political chronology that we discussed in the previous chapter. And, as in that case, we believe that the radicality of this approach in Laclau is limited by his own category of hegemony. Why? In order to answer, we must first consider in more detail how Laclau theorises the *object a*.

First, Laclau argues that in psychoanalysis, the *object a* is defined as a part of the body that represents its totality (this is a questionable reading of the theory, but we'll leave that point aside for the moment). This formulation would connect the *object a* with Laclau's other theory of the nodal point or the floating signifier (later the empty signifier), which constitutes an (impossible) social order. In other words, we are dealing here with a hegemonic signifier (the D_1 of the earlier diagram). In fact, in tropological terms, a nodal point should be considered a metaphor, while what Laclau is describing, in the case of the *object a*, is a synecdoche. However, the effect, in this context, is the same. Directly combining the fields of psychoanalysis and politics, Laclau concludes that the *object a* 'is the key element in a social ontology'.[13] He says this because he associates the *object a* with a social order, which, like the *object a* itself, is considered impossible. In this sense, he had prepared the ground for the term *object a* – which he only introduces in his final book, *On Populist Reason* – throughout his oeuvre, since he had always defined society as an 'impossible object'. What he meant was that since society is based on antagonism, it is never fully constituted. Summing up, Laclau states: 'With this we reach a complete explanation of what radical investment means: making an object the embodiment of a mythical fullness. Affect (that is, enjoyment) is the very essence of investment.'[14] From here on, however, the issue becomes more knotty.

Given the importance that hegemony has always had in Laclau's work, it is not surprising that when he finally introduced the concept of the *object a*, he would try to make it compatible with that theory. Rather than just make the two ideas compatible, however, he ends up assimilating them completely. He says: 'The logic of the *objet petit a* and the hegemonic logic are not just similar: they are simply identical.'[15] Why does he reach this conclusion? We have already explained that Laclau considers that, like hegemony, the term *object a* describes the moment of an encounter between the two aspects of meaning mentioned earlier. This idea is set out in the following comment, which begins with a direct reference to the psychoanalytic field:

> The mythical wholeness of the mother/child dyad, corresponds to the unreached fullness evoked – as its opposite – by the dislocations brought about by the unfulfilled demands. The aspiration to that fullness or wholeness does not, however, simply disappear; it is transferred to partial objects which are the objects of the drives. In political terms, that is exactly what I have called a hegemonic relation: a certain particularity which assumes the role of an impossible universality.[16]

He also writes: 'hegemony is nothing more than the investment, in a partial object, of a fullness which will always evade us because it is purely mythical'.[17] A very important result of these ideas is that they make the object into a *name*. Laclau says:

> Embodying something can only mean giving a *name* to what is being embodied; but, since what is embodied is an impossible fullness, something which has no independent consistency of its own, the 'embodying' entity becomes the full object of cathectic investment.[18]

Or: 'In this way, the partial object ceases to be a partiality evoking a totality, and becomes – using our earlier terminology – the *name* of that totality.'[19] The fact that the *object a qua* name possesses the characteristic of condensing other signifiers is also expressed when Laclau assimilates it to the Lacanian concept of the *point de capiton*, which Lacan conceived in the same way. He says: 'According to Žižek, the quilting point (the *point de capiton*) whose name brings about the unity of a discursive formation – Lacan's *objet petit a* – has no positive identity of its own.'[20] What is the problem that we see with all this?

The first point is that no true Lacanian could accept these glosses. They are equivalent to saying that the S_1 – the master signifier – is identical to the *object a*. If this were so, Lacan's theory of the four discourses – cited in the previous chapter – would collapse, and rapidly so, since this theory depends on a clear distinction being maintained between the two elements. The more urgent problem here (although it is also the product of Laclau's imprecise reading of Lacan) is that the temporal aspect that Laclau sees – correctly – as the most radical aspect of the category of affect, since it specifically refers to political innovation, is completely truncated if it is reduced to a game between the two dimensions of language. In what sense? We have already explained this point: the hegemonic game implies a closure of the field of meaning, not its opening. Therefore, in the same way that we argued in the previous chapter that Laclau makes an illegitimate short-circuit between myth and imaginary, here it seems that he wants to link the 'miracle' of affect directly with the authoritarian power of the social *ego*, which makes no sense at all. What conception of affect, then, is compatible with the ontological premises of our own argument? First, we must ask, what is there in the *object a* that escapes the conceptual reduction presented by Laclau? We must now return to Lacan.

Affect without hegemony

The concept of the *object a* is very complex and has many aspects. It contains elements that correspond with, for example, the three fundamental registers of psychoanalysis that Lacan identified: the imaginary, the symbolic and the real. Hence in Lacan one finds the object of the (imaginary) phantasy, the object(-cause) of desire (which works at the symbolic level) and the object of (real) *jouissance*. We consider that this third aspect is probably the most original and interesting, and that it goes beyond the Laclauian version of the concept. Why? After all, Laclau also associates the *object a* with the real of the drives, which is precisely what he means by the word 'affect'. To explain what Laclau fails to capture, we believe that it is necessary to consider Lacan's formulae of sexuation.[21] What do these consist of?

In the formulae of sexuation (Figure 3.1), two different subjective positions are presented, one on either side of the diagram: the masculine on the left and the feminine on the right. We are going to focus here on the upper part of the diagram, which is more relevant to us than the lower part (except to comment that – as can be seen – the *object a* is present towards the bottom).

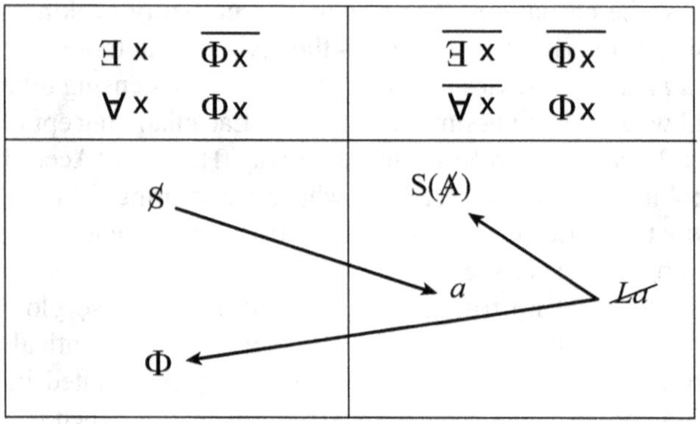

Figure 3.1 The formulae of sexuation.

In each part of the upper section of this diagram, there are two logical formulations that must be considered together, even though they are contraries. On the masculine side we find the following propositions: There exists a *jouissance* that is not phallic *jouissance* $\left(\exists x\, \overline{\phi x}\right)$ /All *jouissance* is phallic *jouissance* ($\forall x\, \phi x$). On the feminine side, we see these: There is no *jouissance* that is not phallic *jouissance* $\left(\overline{\exists x\, \phi x}\right)$ /Not all *jouissance* is phallic *jouissance* $\left(\overline{\forall x}\, \phi x\right)$. The alert reader will already have noticed that the x, in the formulas, is *jouissance* (affect), while the Phi (Φ) is the phallus. It should be noted that the words masculine and feminine, here, do not describe biological factors. In this sense, any 'human being' could fit into either of the two sides, depending on their subjective position.

The first conclusion that can be drawn from these formulae is that the male subjective position is the one that assumes that all its *jouissance* will be phallic *jouissance*, on condition that there exists at least one example of *jouissance* that escapes this logic. It could be added that Lacan considers phallic *jouissance* to be essentially masturbatory, in the sense of repetitive; in the same vein, he occasionally described it as an 'idiotic' *jouissance*. These descriptions are actually effects of the 'limited' character of this *jouissance*. The second conclusion is that the feminine subjective position is that which assumes that although there is no exception to phallic *jouissance*, there is also a realm of *jouissance* that has nothing to do with it and which *jouit* (enjoys) beyond the phallus. These ideas are very difficult to process, but the deduction that we propose to make from them is that the feminine subjective position has access to a register of jouissance that the masculine cannot reach, even though the 'substance' in question, in both cases, is the same. In other words, affect has two different modalities (both based on the immanence of its own field). In Lacan's project, these two modalities are called phallic *jouissance* and feminine *jouissance*, which he sometimes refers to as Other *jouissance*. Why do we consider all this to be so important?

It is noteworthy that Lacan understands feminine *jouissance* as the catalyst for the miraculous – the realisation of the impossible – which we have already discussed. Why? The key here is that the abyss of Other *jouissance* (which is inseparable from the 'abyss' of sexual difference itself) precipitates the production of *singularities*: what Lacan calls the 'one-by-one' of women.[22] In other words, the 'not-All (is phallic *jouissance*)', which is specific to the feminine side of the formulae, opens up the possibility of 'individual' (singular) experiences of *jouissance* that are not reducible to any ordering – neither aggregative, nor condensatory – of the kind that occurs on the masculine side. In fact, the ineffable character of 'feminine *jouissance*s *necessitates* a subjective production of this type. This can be considered an experience of the 'pure contingency' we were discussing earlier on. It also opens up the (paradoxical) possibility of what we have called *plural singularities*. We have tried various times to show how these singularities exceed any attempt to close the fields within which they might emerge. In sum, what we are accusing Laclau of is ignoring the theoretical productivity of feminine *jouissance*. Could it be argued that this register, of Other *jouissance*, is precisely what he has in mind when he speaks of a radical investment: something like an affective excess? It seems that Laclau himself saw it this way. If so, it must be said that his theory lacks precision, since in that case it would also be necessary to explain the role that *phallic jouissance* would play in the picture. Again, if Laclau intends to assimilate *jouissance* – affect – to hegemony, whatever he does he will end up losing one of its registers, according to Lacan's theorisation of it. The most probable result is that he will lose that part that produces *singularities*. In this sense, we believe the *jouissance* that fits best with the theory of hegemony presented by Laclau is phallic *jouissance*. After all, in such a modality we are dealing with a limited *jouissance* (unlike feminine *jouissance*, which is unlimited), which is therefore consubstantial (to use Laclau's own term) with signification, and furthermore that, via a constitutive exception, it is constituted as an exclusive unity: what we have previously described as a replete social formation, albeit one that is founded on the suppression of its void. In this sense, hegemony is a process that is hardly miraculous, to return to the earlier term.

For a renewed theory of populism, then, we must now rely on 'Other affect', which may also include popular enthusiasm. This factor opens the door to unknown political possibilities: singularities, which before being experienced would have been considered impossible. Our conclusion thus confirms the theses of the liberals, mentioned at the beginning of this chapter: enthusiasm is a necessary part of populism. We would only add that, unlike the liberals, we welcome this aspect. To reach this happy conclusion, however, we have once again had to separate the populist logic from that of hegemony. Finally, we could mention that there are people who have tried to combine the fields of politics and psychoanalysis directly, at this level. In fact, Laclau did the same, even if he did not seriously investigate the field of Other *jouissance*, as we have already explained. Other authors have argued that, given the connection with Other *jouissance*, populism should be considered 'feminine', even 'feminist'.[23] We will not go into this topic now, since it is very complex (and theoretically controversial). We will simply move on to the next topic we would like to discuss, namely that of the distinction between truth and post-truth.

Notes

1 www.prospectmagazine.co.uk/magazine/is-reason-the-slave-of-the-passions-philosophy-hume.
2 Jacques Lacan, *The Seminar of Jacques Lacan, Book 1 – Freud's Papers on Technique 1953–1954* (London: Norton), 1991, p. 55.
3 For example: Simon Critchley and Oliver Marchart (Eds.), *Laclau – A Critical Reader* (London: Routledge), 2004, p. 299.
4 Simon Critchley and Oliver Marchart (Eds.), *Laclau – A Critical Reader* (London: Routledge), 2004, p. 326.
5 Simon Critchley and Oliver Marchart (Eds.), *Laclau – A Critical Reader* (London: Routledge), 2004, pp. 302–303, 326.
6 Simon Critchley and Oliver Marchart (Eds.), *Laclau – A Critical Reader* (London: Routledge), 2004, p. 303.
7 Ernesto Laclau, *On Populist Reason* (London: Verso), 2005, p. 115.
8 E.g., Ernesto Laclau, *Emancipation(s)* (London: Verso), 1996, pp. 78, 81.
9 Judith Butler, Ernesto Laclau and Slavoj Žižek, *Contingency, Hegemony and Universality – Contemporary Dialogues on the Left* (London: Verso), 2000, p. 84.
10 See: Jacques Lacan, *The Seminar of Jacques Lacan, Book X – Anxiety* (Cambridge: Polity), 2015, p. 131.
11 Ernesto Laclau, *On Populist Reason* (London: Verso), 2005, p. 116.
12 See: Ernesto Laclau, *Emancipation(s)* (London: Verso), 1996; Ernesto Laclau, *New Reflections on the Revolution of Our Time* (London: Verso), 1990.
13 Ernesto Laclau, *On Populist Reason* (London: Verso), 2005, p. 115.
14 Ernesto Laclau, *On Populist Reason* (London: Verso), 2005, p. 115.
15 Ernesto Laclau, *On Populist Reason* (London: Verso), 2005, p. 116.
16 Ernesto Laclau, *On Populist Reason* (London: Verso), 2005, pp. 114–115.
17 Ernesto Laclau, *On Populist Reason* (London: Verso), 2005, p. 116, emphasis in the original.
18 Ernesto Laclau, *On Populist Reason* (London: Verso), 2005, p. 119, emphasis in the original.
19 Ernesto Laclau, *On Populist Reason* (London: Verso), 2005, p. 114.
20 Ernesto Laclau, *On Populist Reason* (London: Verso), 2005, p. 103.
21 See: Jacques Lacan, *The Seminar of Jacques Lacan, Book 20 – On Feminine Sexuality, the Limits of Love and Knowledge, 1972–1973: Encore* (London: Norton), 1999.
22 Jacques Lacan, *The Seminar of Jacques Lacan, Book 20 – On Feminine Sexuality, the Limits of Love and Knowledge, 1972–1973: Encore* (London: Norton), 1999, p. 10.
23 See for example: Mercedes de Franciso, De la angustia a la izquierda lacaniana, Paloma Blanco Díaz, Lógica de la posición femenina y emancipación: El psicoanalálisis como factor de la política, and Luciana Cadahia, Hacia una política 'antígonista', in: Timothy Appleton and José Alberto Raymondi (Eds.), *Lacan en las lógicas de la emancipación – En torno a textos de Jorge Alemán* (Malagá: Miguel Gomez), 2018, pp. 223–233, 297–306, 307–319.

Chapter 4

Is populism post-truth?

Populism is often associated with post-truth culture. The *Oxford English Dictionary* definition of 'post-truth' (which it chose as its word of the year in 2016) is: 'Relating to or denoting circumstances in which objective facts are less influential in shaping public opinion than appeals to emotion and personal belief'.[1] Once again: subjectivity and affect. Perhaps the most obvious manifestation of this culture is – what has been called – 'fake news'. This concept has spread so quickly that now those who have been accused of promoting this kind of fake news – Donald Trump, for example – repeat the same accusation against their own enemies (Trump even said, at one point, that he himself had invented the word 'fake' to describe the phenomenon), and thus we enter a nihilistic vicious circle.[2] These new concepts seem to have their origins in the Anglophone world. Perhaps it is to be appreciated that these territories have finally begun to take seriously the contingency of knowledge, even in its empirical sense. On the European continent, this step was taken a long time ago. What we want to defend in this chapter, however, is that populism should not be associated with post-truth but rather with *truth*. When we use the latter word, what do we have in mind?

We have just made reference to developments in European intellectual culture. Let's give an example. In France, since 1960, the entire genre of 'post-structuralist' thought began to relativise, partly through a process of historical contextualisation, every kind of scientific knowledge. Authors like Michel Foucault and Jacques Derrida began to show that any 'truth claim' will have (transcendental?) conditions of existence and that in this sense, such claims cannot be accepted at face value. Despite what we said before, there was actually a similar movement in the English-speaking world: the argument of a Thomas Kuhn, for example, or a Richard Rorty. In the face of so much 'scepticism', some began to wonder if it would be possible to continue using the word 'truth', or if it would be better to abandon it altogether. There was another French thinker, however, who unreservedly asserted the importance of this word. We have already mentioned him: Jacques Lacan. Actually, what Lacan did was to bring an important nuance into the post-structuralist debate. In the first place, he accepted the premise of the contingency of knowledge; and precisely for this reason, he argued that the time had finally come to embrace the category of truth. In what sense?

DOI: 10.4324/9781003431916-7

Instead of considering the truth as something 'objective', Lacan assumed that it concerned the subject. One can see that he had the opposite philosophy to those who write for the *Oxford English Dictionary*: for him, the subjective experience is much more valid, on a material level, than the objective one. Lacan thought that the truth was something that sets the subject in motion in the first place (it is its 'cause', to use his own terminology) but that such a subject would also have problems accepting it. The origin of this idea is clearly Freud's theory of castration. Lacan adds that if the 'unveiling' of the truth by a subject is possible, it must be considered a *process*, in the same way that we said earlier that affective investment implies a temporal process. Lacan considered this process of revealing the truth as constitutive of truth itself. This idea echoes Heidegger's discussion of the Greek word *aletheia* (disclosure, precisely), which he also associated with the theme of truth. Lacan was heavily influenced by this discussion. Another way to summarise these ideas would be to say that for Lacan, truth is a (subjective) *act*. In the same sense, truth can be considered a 'construction', which the subject carries out precisely by adhering to its own non-being (its castration). Now, the subject that Lacan had in mind, here, was obviously the subject of the clinic. He considered that the process of discovering the truth, on the part of the subject, was equivalent to that of psychoanalysis itself. What happens, however, with a different type of subject? The subject that most interests us is of course that which is found in the field of politics, which we have called 'the people'. To consider the relationship between such a subject and truth, we propose to return to the work of a thinker who was highly influenced by Lacan, but who also thinks politics in detail: Alain Badiou.

We have already said that the central category of Badiou's project is the *event*. Let us remember that an event produces an antagonism, in a sense that we have associated with populism. In fact, an event constitutes a *temporalisation* of antagonism, in a way that – for example – Laclau's theory of hegemony is capable of conceiving but not embracing. The most important thing here, however, is that Badiou argues that an event produces a truth. In what sense? For Badiou, an event is located on what he calls 'an evental site', which is adjacent to the void of a situation of being. An important aspect of this theory is that an event includes not only the elements of the multiple that is this void but also itself. Perhaps we could call this the tautology of truth, which is also present in the Lacanian version of the concept, according to which a subject produces the very truth that caused it in the first place. Badiou explains this paradox as follows: self-inclusion is ontologically prohibited, so truth must be considered the result of a *decision*, on the part of its subject.[3]

Could this be considered a 'decisionistic' position, according to which the relevant subjective act is thought of as something purely voluntary? It could not, precisely because the void that founds this decision is *real*, even though this aspect does not materialise until the decision on its existence has already been made. And it is indeed possible never to make this decision. Is a decision in this sense something unique? According to Badiou, a decision should in fact be divided into two moments, the combination of which he calls an *intervention*. The first decision a subject must make is to name the event. Actually, this is simply the first way of declaring that an event has taken place. The second form that an intervention assumes is when a subject takes responsibility for the way in which the name of the event 'circulates' in the relevant situation. This process consists of carrying out a series of tests – which Badiou calls *inquiries* – of the different parts of a situation in order to ascertain their relation to the evental site.[4] Badiou describes this process as deductive, in the sense of demonstrative, and conceptually coherent. He adds that the same process establishes, as it goes along, a norm of connection between the multiples it is testing. Badiou will add that as a result of this process, two types of information are produced. What are they?

Badiou shares with Lacan and Heidegger the idea that, under normal circumstances (that is, a situation), the truth remains hidden. This is why he calls it *indiscernible*.[5] He also inherits from Lacan the idea that truth, on this definition, is opposed to knowledge, which is what Badiou believes constitutes a situation. He calls the sum of the knowledge of a situation its 'encyclopedia'.[6] He characterises this type of knowledge as *veridical*, to distinguish it from truth as such. Again, what separates these two categories is that encyclopaedic information – unlike that of truth – does not include (at least) one sub-multiple that is indiscernible from the point of view of its situation. Badiou calls a set that conforms to this last criterion *generic*. It is so called in part because insofar as it belongs to a situation, it does so in an absolutely insubstantial way – belonging *qua* belonging, one could say – and also because the fact that this type of set presents the truth of a situation means that it is distributed between all parts of the latter. The corollary is that the generic set can be glimpsed and declared from the point of view of any multiple of this situation. In this sense, it is available to anyone, even if they do not discern it in all times and places. For the same reason, Badiou says that: 'The generic is *egalitarian*': it is 'for-all'.[7] Logically, the word 'generic' can also be used to describe the truth that an event produces. Another important term in Badiou, which is closely related to his concept of the generic set, is *forcing*. What does the latter consist of?

The term forcing has two aspects. First, it denominates the process of obliging a situation to accommodate a generic set. At another point, Badiou refers to this process as the passage from representation – in the sense that, in a given situation, a (generic) member of the sub-multiples of the evental site is represented – to presentation, or pure belonging. More simply, he will say that it indicates the transition from inclusion to belonging. The second important aspect of forcing it is that it involves an anticipation. In what sense? Following the emergence of an event, the inquiries that continue to constitute it not only verify the positive (or negative) connection that certain ideas or affirmations – that is, certain multiples – have with said event, but at the same time constitute a wager on the significance these statements might have in a future situation *that also includes the event*. In this sense, forcing represents a sort of temporal loop between the present and the future. Badiou avers that this process postulates the 'parallel' existence of situations in which certain statements are true and others in which they are not.[8] This echoes Rancière's distinction between actual and hypothetical situations, which we discussed in the first chapter. In this sense, the concept of forcing in Badiou introduces a moment of undecidability to the situation itself. Badiou describes this as the passage 'from the indiscernible to the undecidable'.[9] After all, what is a (political) antagonism if not this? The 'loop' of forcing also echoes the future anterior – what will have been – of the subject, which Lacan had already identified as its 'logical time', or – alternatively – what he called 'the assertion of anticipated certainty'.[10]

There is much to take in here. We have already explained that we do not accept all the theoretical moves that Badiou makes, especially his articulation between a philosophical ontology and a 'social ontology'. On the other hand, his theoretical description of the way in which a truth may spread through a situation seems very important to us. The key point is that Badiou connects truth with a political antagonism, via an event. This is especially important to us because antagonism is at the core of our definition of populism. We would not want to place too much emphasis, at this time, on the nameable dimension of the event. Sometimes Badiou's event risks coming across as monolithic (Laclau understood this very well), and we don't want to be accused of treating it the same way. Again, we prefer to focus simply on the antagonism that an event brings with it, and the truth that this produces. To us, it seems crucial to assume that truth lies in the decision to separate oneself from the encyclopaedia of veridical knowledge that is found in a situation. It must also be emphasised that this should be done in a radical, singular and unexpected way, which are indeed the properties of an event. As Badiou puts it: 'a truth is always what makes a hole in knowledge'.[11] In this sense, adhering to the truth can be considered the task of an 'interventionist' subject, to play on another Badiouian term. It is probably also important to affirm that when (political) truth circulates in a social situation, it establishes its own (deductive) logic. Additionally, we believe that truth can be considered generic, and, in the same sense, it imposes a relationship of equality between those who advocate for it. Finally, we think that it should be accepted that forcing a truth, within a situation, involves making a wager, with respect to another type of future situation in which this truth is definitively present, or, to put it another way, in which the truth has been 'demonstrated'.

The overarching conclusion here is that it is no longer necessary to be afraid of the word 'truth' in a political context. It might even be something that is present in many common and everyday situations, just so long as they contain an element that has been separated, in a punctual way, from veridical knowledge. In other words, a generic element. If it is accepted, then, that this form of truth is associated with social antagonism, it can be deduced that *populism is based on truth*. When we speak of truth, here, what we have in mind is a *process*, or a subjective production. At no point is it an 'empirical' truth. Indeed, it can be said that truth begins where the empirical ends. Here a doubt will surely arise. If it is the case that populism is based on truth, why has the term been so naturally associated, in recent times, with post-truth? Sometimes, populism appears to be a synonym of post-truth because even simulacrous populism – that of the right-wing – recognises the real of antagonism, although it subsequently tries radically to hide it. In the same sense, the condition for there to be post-truth is that there must first be a truth. We assume, then, that in the same way that left-wing populism can be perverted and made into right-wing populism, false conclusions can also be drawn from the fact that a situation contains a void, to put it once again in Badiouian terms.

Is the view of truth that we have presented here compatible with the theory of hegemony? Since we are associating truth with antagonism, and considering that hegemony also contains this element, it should in principle be possible to think them together. On the other hand, it seems symptomatic to us that, in general terms, the defenders of hegemony prefer not to talk about the issue of truth. Why do we think this happens? Firstly, it could be a consequence of the structuralist influence on that theory; that is, structuralists tend to assume that what we usually call truth is a mirage, due to what they see as the linguistic mediation of reality. But we think this idea could be made a bit more specific. It seems to us that there is an irreducible uncertainty, in the structuralist *Weltanschauung*, regarding the division of labour between the metaphorical and the metonymical axes of language. We consider that this uncertainty is, in turn, an effect of a(n albeit implicit) postulate of full speech. These two ideas correspond to the criticisms that we have already made of the theory of hegemony: its indecision regarding the exact location of a social antagonism, precisely as an effect of its assumption of the possibility of a social field that is not only delimited but also, in some sense, full. Now we may move on to the next relevant question: how does the question of leadership affect what we have argued so far?

Notes

1 www.politico.eu/article/post-truth-enters-oxford-english-dictionary/.
2 www.independent.co.uk/news/world/americas/donald-trump-takes-credit-for-inventing-the-word-fake-a7989221.html.
3 Alain Badiou, *Being and Event* (London: Continuum), 2005, p. 190.
4 Alain Badiou, *Being and Event* (London: Continuum), 2005, p. 234.
5 Alain Badiou, *Being and Event* (London: Continuum), 2005, p. 342.
6 Alain Badiou, *Being and Event* (London: Continuum), 2005, p. 327.
7 Alain Badiou, *Being and Event* (London: Continuum), 2005, p. 409.
8 Alain Badiou, *Being and Event* (London: Continuum), 2005, p. 414.
9 Alain Badiou, *Being and Event* (London: Continuum), 2005, p. 410.
10 Jacques Lacan, *Écrits* (London: Norton), 2006, p. 161.
11 Alain Badiou, *Being and Event* (London: Continuum), 2005, p. 327.

Chapter 5

What makes a populist leader?

First, we must ask ourselves, here, what leadership consists of from the point of view of hegemony (of the populist variety). Laclau and Mouffe have written almost nothing on this subject, so, in order to answer the question, we may have to speculate a bit. It is logical that a 'hegemonic' leader is a person who would be capable of representing and consolidating various popular demands (or antagonisms). To put it in terms of Lacan's discourses, one is dealing with the incarnation of a master signifier, now added – maybe – to the 'surplus' requirement that such a leader be a figure that inspires a popular (affective) excitement that, according to Laclau, would correspond to the dimension of 'emptiness' that such a signifier supposedly contains. At this point, all our criticisms of the category of hegemony could be reiterated. However, it will be asked what model of leadership we wish to substitute for that of the hegemonic perspective, all the while taking into account our own theorisation of populism. Before responding, it will probably be necessary to develop in more detail the question of *ethics*. We have seen that Laclau occasionally refers to this issue, but we have also argued that his analysis is limited, once again by his own theory of hegemony. To open up a new horizon, we again propose to focus, in the following discussion of the topic, on the Lacan–Badiou nexus: Lacan will provide the initial theoretical inspiration and Badiou will extend the object of this theory to politics (among other things).

The populist ethic

There are several points that need to be explained immediately. The first is that when we discuss ethics, we are not talking about an abstract set of norms that could be applied in all situations. For example, when people try to introduce an ethic of non-violence in political situations, we do not consider this type of argument relevant, as desirable as it might seem, since it imposes an arbitrary and precipitate limit on politics itself. It can therefore be deduced that ethics is a second-degree topic. In what sense? In the case of politics, for example, we believe that what is needed is an ethics *of* politics. In other words, we require an ethics that is always at a distance from the *thing*. In fact, this is the precise formulation of Badiou, in his book on the subject.[1] What would such an ethics consist of? Given that we indeed

DOI: 10.4324/9781003431916-8

want to avoid an ethical form that limits politics – by transcending it – it would probably be better to go in the other direction and assume that what we require is precisely an ethics that keeps a political sequence going, that allows it to develop. This explains why both Badiou and Lacan make the idea of *persevering* their fundamental ethical proposal. In the case of Lacan, his basic formula is that one should not give ground relative to one's desire.[2] This seems to us to be another way of saying 'persevere'. Desire, in Lacan's formulation, has to do with what Badiou has called the indiscernible (of a situation), in the sense of that truth that corresponds to a subject for whom such a truth is difficult to recognise and assume. For his part, Badiou calls the aspect of perseverance: *fidelity* (to the event; that is, to the construction of an antagonism).[3] This last term could perhaps be explored a little more.

At first sight, Badiou's concept of fidelity is quite simple. Essentially, it consists of the subject of an antagonism continuing in its being. Badiou also argues, however, that fidelity has dimensions of 'militancy' and 'discipline', and will add that it has two main deviations (as always, in politics?): *dogmatism*, which consists of over-institutionalising the event that fidelity has produced; and *spontaneism*, which consists of over-particularising the event.[4] Later on, Badiou adds another figure of deviationist fidelity, which he calls *terroristic* (much later, he will call it 'obscure'), namely that which opts for the plenitude of a situation after having glimpsed its emptiness.[5] In Chapter 2, we called this – following Badiou himself – a *simulacrum*. It evokes the 'terrorist' dimension of the ultra-right. Beyond such nuances, Badiou begins to search, at a certain point, for a specific example of an ethical subject, one that might conform to his own theoretical premises. The person he finally chooses is *Saint Paul*, saying:

> For me, Paul is a poet-thinker of the event, as well as one who practices and states the invariant traits of what can be called the militant figure. He brings forth the entirely human connection, whose destiny fascinates me, between the general idea of a rupture, an overturning, and that of a thought-practice that is this rupture's subjective materiality.
>
> If today I wish to retrace in a few pages the singularity of this connection in Paul, it is probably because there is currently a widespread search for a new militant figure – even if it takes the form of denying its possibility – called upon to succeed the one installed by Lenin and the Bolsheviks at the beginning of the century, which can be said to have been that of the party militant.[6]

It is curious that Badiou feels the need to go back so far in history to find an alternative to the form of the modern political party, but there it is. What specific aspects does Badiou draw from the figure of Paul, at this level? Before answering, we must summarise the relevant doctrine.

First, Badiou makes reference to what he calls the 'law' that Paul invented in order for a fidelity to be established.[7] What is this law supposed to consist of? The best-known part of it is probably its *universalism*. Badiou sums this point up by saying that Paul subtracts truth from 'the communitarian grasp'.[8] Perhaps the first affirmation of this universalism is Paul's monumental phrase from Galatians: 'There is neither Jew nor Greek, there is neither bond nor free, there is neither male nor female: for ye are all one in Christ Jesus.' Badiou deduces from this formula that Paul can be considered a thinker of *absolute equality*. What other traits does he see in Paul? It is well known that Paul sums up Christian doctrine in one single point: accepting the resurrection of Jesus Christ. He also perceives that the fact that Christ is the son of God creates – what Badiou calls – an irreducible *filiation* between those who believe in his resurrection.[9] The important point is that the condition of Paul's universalism is precisely this belief, as can be observed in the previous comment from Galatians ('ye are all one in Christ Jesus'). To say that this is a 'belief' does not imply that it can be considered a mere 'concept', or – even worse – an ideology (as the – structuralist – theory of hegemony would be obliged to conclude). Rather, it should be understood as a principle that is realised at the very moment it is accepted. Thus, it represents an example of the short circuit between belief and being that Badiou describes, in *Being and Event*, as *forcing* (see the previous chapter). For Badiou, the three aspects mentioned – universalism, egalitarianism, and fraternity – designate Paul as a *Communist* thinker. Badiou is not the first person to come to this conclusion; he himself claims to have partly inherited it from Pier Paolo Pasolini, the filmmaker, who wrote (but never shot) a film about Pablo, in which he argued the same thing.[10] For our part, we are more interested in connecting this theory with that of populism, but we will return to this in a moment.

In truth, the only thing that has been demonstrated so far is that Paul's ideas are compatible with various theoretical principles found in Badiou. It is precisely this that allows us, however, to move on to the specifically ethical aspect of his leadership. Perhaps the key moment in relation to this dimension, in Badiou's monograph, is the following quote from Paul: 'We have become, and are now, as the refuse of the world, the offscouring of all things.'[11] Badiou will add that, by associating themselves with the real of a situation, subjects of truth, like Paul, do not fit into this world (or situation): they are *leftovers*, so to speak (as in the title of the famous HBO series). It is in this sense that they can be considered refuse, or 'excrement', to use a more clinical word. Badiou also makes a connection with psychoanalysis here; he associates the quote from Paul with the ethics of the Lacanian psychoanalyst. What does this have to do with it? Let's go back to Freud.

Ethical leadership

In his essay *Analysis Terminable and Interminable*, Freud argues that there are three impossible professions: educating, governing and psychoanalysing. The idea is that those who work in these fields, whether they do their job well or not, are going to find themselves emotionally rejected at the end of the process. This is so because they are mere agents of change and little else; they are – so to speak – catalysts, who are not going to share in the glory that they have contributed to building, although they will indeed share in the failure, if things don't work out!

Freud adds that an analyst who has already gone through their own analysis will interfere less in the progress of an analysis with a patient of theirs in the future. Having gone through analysis implies having fewer defects and being in a position of (moral) 'superiority', to put it in Freud's 19th-century bourgeois terms.[12] The important thing about this idea is that if the analyst has already been treated, they will be more capable of assuming their own position as a rejected product of the process ('refuse'). This is the key ethical point. A 'well-analysed' psychoanalyst will be able to accept his own rejection at the end of his labours. Lacan, for his part, connects this last idea with the figure of the saint. Why? His idea is that a saint has to accept in advance that his character will be abused and broken during the process of being a witness to, and agent of, a specific truth, and Lacan thinks that this description can also be applied to the analyst. To put it in classically psychoanalytic terms: a saint has no *ego* or, better put, they have learned to separate themselves from their *ego*. In fact, this last idea, which arises above all in the late Lacan, was foreshadowed in one of his earliest seminars – the seventh – in which he presented his ethical exemplar, *Antigone*.[13]

Lacan believes that Antigone is important because she knows what she has to do (bury her brother), and she also knows that this act is completely prohibited by the laws of the state but she does it anyway. In this sense, Antigone does not give up on her desire, to express it in Lacan's terms. To perform this final ethical act, however, Antigone also, in some way, has to desire her own disappearance, or even her destruction as a person (this is the tragic dimension of her story). All these characteristics, then, are ways of highlighting the fidelity of the saint: their constancy, and their faith that what is being done *must* be done. By someone. The saint therefore chooses to be this 'someone', this anonymous person (to use Badiou's term) who is not defined by anything other than their fidelity to the event.[14] It is clear that these conclusions have directly political implications. However, the fact that someone decides to act ethically surely does not imply that a political intervention will take place? After all, politics is ultimately a collective act; one assumes that it is not a question of mere 'individual' interventions.

The most notable thing about Paul is that he had followers (without them, the Christian religion would not exist!). This is reflected in his epistolary way of writing. Here we come to the question of the connection between the character of Paul and the Christians of his time. To guide us in this matter, we will turn our attention to the famous essay by Louis Althusser, *Ideology and Ideological State Apparatuses*. In this work, Althusser presents several original theses, among them, the following: 'all ideology hails or interpellates concrete individuals as concrete subjects'.[15] The word 'interpellates' is key here. Althusser argues that when an authority figure addresses a person, the person in question may identify with this address. The – rather theatrical – example that he introduces in his essay is that of a policeman who yells at somebody in the street: 'Hey, you there!', thus obliging that person to turn through 180 degrees to look at him.[16] In this semi-circular turn, the individual becomes a subject, according to Althusser. The model for this scene is clearly Lacan's 'mirror stage' and the relationship between a baby, who looks at itself in a mirror for the first time, and the mother (or other adult) who stands behind this baby, inviting it to identify with its own image. The problem with Althusser's example, from our point of view, is precisely that it only covers 'imaginary' relationships, that is, those that are extrapolated from the image in the mirror and concern the unifying process of the *ego*. Althusser associates ideology itself with this aspect, and he is probably right to do so. Our argument, however, is that a subject is not reducible to subject positions within an order of authority, with its prerogative of unification and the accompanying ideological apparatuses. This would represent the orthodox hegemonic logic. As we explained earlier, we believe that a subject is only born at the moment in which it identifies with the *gap* in this very order (thus producing an antagonism), something that hegemony can never locate with any degree of certainty. Nevertheless, we wonder whether via the 'ethical' figure of the saint there arises the possibility of a different type of inter-pellation, namely the moment in which a subject identifies with the *subjectivity* of another subject of the gap. What does this mean?

Perhaps it could simply be speculated that a true leader, due to their ethical dis-position, sets an example for the way in which other subjects – their followers, for example – should behave. The paradigmatic example of such a leader is, again, the saint; this is why saints have so much cultural value. Perhaps this is what ultimately explains why Badiou chose the example of Saint Paul. When Paul writes the epistles, he is not trying to influence his followers regarding his ideology, nor is he trying to exert his power. He simply relates certain things, a process that permits him to dem-onstrate to his followers his own 'disinterested-interest' (as Badiou calls it) in the face of the event, thus providing such followers with an ethical(-political?) model that they can imitate.[17] In this sense, it can be said that the followers connect with the subjectivity of the leader, rather than with their message or their unifying figure as such. Rancière, for his part, has described this phenomenon in the following way:

> The propagator no longer seeks to reconstitute a small band. As an anonymous and isolated individual, he sets off to share the spark of the spirit of revolt – of the spirit, period – with a crowd capable of catching fire precisely insofar as it is not a gathering of families, societies, classes or corporations but a pure col-lection of sensitive individuals: that is, a mass fusing through the energy of its molecules, with which the rebel makes contact at one point in a relationship without reciprocity.[18]

It could be added that the more successful this type of person is, the more visible they will be, and this in turn can increase their success, and so on. What, then, does all this have to do with populism?

We would like to propose the thesis that the populist leader is indeed a saint, an ethical exemplar for an entire movement. This would explain the 'personalist' touch that populism has, which so scares the liberals. How does this conclusion relate to the rest of our theoretical argument? The key point is that ethical leader-ship, as we have described it here, is the only one that is capable of embracing an antagonism in its pure singularity. In fact, the two factors go hand in hand: it is only possible to be truly faithful to something that you would not believe twice.[19] And the absolute singularity of an antagonism is, of course, the central part of our definition of populism. These conclusions rule out a leader who is only capable of linking together different antagonisms, in order to 'seize power' in a specific social field. Such a leader – which would be compatible with the theory of hegemony – would represent something like an imaginary father figure, who manages to bring the whole family together. We, however, would wish to escape from such an oedipal entanglement, thus embracing the sheer equality between a leader and their followers, with regard to a truly singular antagonism. Let us now move on to another topic. In the first chapter of this book, we referred to the question of the nation. Therein we conceded that the defence of the latter should be considered a legitimate political struggle, among others. But it must be recognised that there are many people – even left-wingers – who do not agree with this point. We therefore think it worthwhile to consider this topic in more detail.

Notes

1 Alain Badiou, *Ethics – An Essay on the Understanding of Evil* (London: Verso), 2001, p. 28.
2 Jacques Lacan, *The Seminar of Jacques Lacan, Book 7: The Ethics of Psychoanalysis 1959–1960* (New York: Norton), 1992, p. 319.
3 Alain Badiou, *Being and Event* (London: Continuum), 2005, p. 232.
4 Alain Badiou, *Being and Event* (London: Continuum), 2005, p. 237.
5 Alain Badiou, *Ethics – An Essay on the Understanding of Evil* (London: Verso), 2001, p. 77.
6 Alain Badiou, *Saint Paul – The Foundation of Universalism* (Stanford: Stanford University Press), 2003, p. 2.
7 Alain Badiou, *Saint Paul – The Foundation of Universalism* (Stanford: Stanford University Press), 2003, p. 5.
8 Alain Badiou, *Saint Paul – The Foundation of Universalism* (Stanford: Stanford University Press), 2003, p. 5.
9 Alain Badiou, *Saint Paul – The Foundation of Universalism* (Stanford: Stanford University Press), 2003, p. 69.
10 Alain Badiou, *Saint Paul – The Foundation of Universalism* (Stanford: Stanford University Press), 2003, p. 36.
11 Alain Badiou, *Saint Paul – The Foundation of Universalism* (Stanford: Stanford University Press), 2003, p. 56.
12 Sigmund Freud, *Standard Edition*, Vol. XXIII (London: Hogarth), 2001, p. 248.
13 Jacques Lacan, *The Seminar of Jacques Lacan, Book 7: The Ethics of Psychoanalysis 1959–1960* (New York: Norton), 1992.
14 Alain Badiou, *Saint Paul – The Foundation of Universalism* (Stanford: Stanford University Press), 2003, p. 94.
15 Louis Althusser, *Lenin and Philosophy and Other Essays* (New Delhi: Aakar), 2006, p. 117.
16 Louis Althusser, *Lenin and Philosophy and Other Essays* (New Delhi: Aakar), 2006, p. 118.
17 Alain Badiou, *Ethics – An Essay on the Understanding of Evil* (London: Verso), 2001, p. 69.
18 Jacques Rancière, *Proletarian Nights: The Workers' Dream in Nineteenth-Century France* (London: Verso), 2012, p. 119.
19 The phrase comes from Badiou: 'Love what you will never believe twice' (Alain Badiou, *Theory of the Subject* (London: Bloomsbury), 2013, p. 331.)

Chapter 6

Is there a connection between populism and nationalism?

One of the most common prejudices among today's intellectual classes is the idea that the nation no longer exists, as a valid unit of socio-political analysis. To us, this opinion borders on the delusional. Perhaps we could at least concede that it has two versions, which one would call left- and right-wing. The right-wing version defends the uninterrupted movement of capital, as a way of liberating – supposedly – the peoples of the world. The left-wing version is the same as the right-wing one but it adds a dimension of moral solidarity and the imperative not to behave in a racist manner. It is tempting to call these two positions: right-wing neoliberalism and left-wing neoliberalism. In truth, we think that, despite their official pronunciations on the subject, it is not entirely the case that today's intellectuals believe that nations have been abolished. Rather, they think that they *should be* abolished, which is an entirely different matter. Why do they think so?

Many intellectuals do not like nations because they indeed associate them with racism. The territory where this opinion is most widespread is Europe, and it is true that on that continent, the figure of the nation has a reputation for being racist, for reasons that are probably obvious. Perhaps the main problem in Europe is not really the existence of nations, but instead the fact that such are (relatively) powerful, which is always to be criticised. However, one can deduce from this that there must also be nations in the world that do *not* have so much power. Do they not have the right to assert themselves? It is easy to show that they do. After all, what normal person would not support the national liberation struggles that took place throughout the post-colonial era: Haiti, India, Cuba, Vietnam, Angola, South Africa etc. It could be added that the figure of the 'people' has always been present in these post-colonial struggles. Badiou himself has argued that during the anti-colonial wars it was *necessary* to use this term, since the colonial powers had used other names to refer to the colonised communities: tribes, ethnic groups (savages, one could add).[1] In this sense, defining themselves as a people was a way of the colonised demonstrating their equality with those who colonised them. Perhaps it is no accident that the new populist theory – which has influenced us so much – has its origins in the post-colonial states of Latin America: Argentina above all. What theory underlies these considerations?

DOI: 10.4324/9781003431916-9

Once again, the key point is the antagonistic division of social space. This is shown in Badiou's own theory. It is interesting, for example, that the first political example he provides of his central category of the event, in his masterpiece *Being and Event*, is the French Revolution, which is precisely a *national* revolution.[2] As will be imagined, the relationship between this event and the situation from which it has been subtracted is complex. That revolution can be considered French not just in the sense that it happened within a pre-constituted place called France, but also because France is the name of the place that is retroactively justified – even constituted – by its own event. It can be concluded that there were two Frances at stake, in such a situation. Badiou later commented on this issue in an interview, saying that:

> no category is *in itself* blocked from its possible politicization. Even 'Arab,' even 'Islam,' even 'Jew,' even 'French', can, at a given moment, have a progressive political signification. When de Gaulle addressed the French from London – the French meaning, for him, the resistants – 'French' had a progressive signification, that of anti-Nazi resistance. This proves that these things can change.[3]

In fact, this aspect reaffirms Rancière's theoretical position, which states that literally any social identity can, at a given moment, be subjectified. Badiou has also looked in more detail at the 'popular' dimension of this theory, in an essay published in 2013, called *Twenty-Four Notes on the Uses of the Word 'People'*.

In his essay, Badiou argues that it is still possible today for a people to carry out a national liberation struggle. Under what circumstances? The basic condition, according to Badiou, is that the people in question must be in a *pre-state* situation, i.e. they have not yet created their own state. It is true that the main example that Badiou offers of such a people is the international proletariat; as we explained earlier, for us this attitude reflects a fairly traditional Marxist prejudice. Nevertheless, Badiou does not rule out the possibility that there may currently exist examples of pre-state peoples that effectively are able to resist 'colonial and imperial domination or by the domination of an invader'.[4] It must be recognised that Badiou describes this second example – the wars of national liberation – as a 'transitory' form of the people, while he considers the first example – communism – as its final form. We feel that this addendum is expendable. For us, Brexit contains the same emancipatory potential as any other kind of national liberation struggle, despite the colonial history of the British people themselves. It all depends on what the British themselves choose to do with it.[5] After all, as we have already suggested, it is always possible for one 'people' to oppose another, using the same signifier (the British people against another, purported 'British people'), within their own territory. In fact, in order to maintain this theoretical line, we think that it is necessary to supplement theories such as those of Badiou or Rancière. How so?

Badiou would describe his philosophical project as 'immanentist', unlike the theories that he considers to be based on 'transcendence'. This is very relevant to his theory of the event, since the latter is an element that, he insists, should not be thought of as something that 'transcends' a situation, although it is indeed separated from it. One implication of this idea is that the resources – the 'power' – of an event do not come from outside: rather, they are intrinsic to it; once again, they are 'immanent'. This is where we feel we can extend our theoretical metaphors slightly. We propose to call the factor we have just described *sovereignty*, a term that, it is true, does not usually arise in post-Althusserian thought. It is a complex word, with a long history. We believe that in its essence it raises the issue of making do with one's own subjective resources, which are absolutely (but not transcendentally) separable from other forms. In the same sense, we think that it is possible to distinguish this term from its purely legal connotations. The exact distinction would be between the indivisibility – in our terms, the singularity – of power, versus divisible powers, which are legal ones. This distinction in fact forms a very traditional part of the concept of sovereignty.[6]

An interesting reference here is Georges Bataille. Bataille once commented that: 'The sovereignty I speak of has little to do with the sovereignty of States, as international law defines it. I speak in general of an aspect that is opposed to the servile and the subordinate.' He adds:

I shall always be concerned, however it may seem, with the apparently lost sovereignty to which the beggar can sometimes be as close as the great nobleman, and from which, as a rule, the bourgeois is voluntarily the most far removed.[7]

This comment returns us to a more Badiouian principle, according to which sovereignty adheres to a void (what has been 'lost', in the preceding quote). In addition, Bataille's pejorative reference to the bourgeois shows the anti-liberal dimension that sovereignty can be said to have. We do not think it is an accident that Bataille comes to this conclusion: he was influenced by Marx, so he understood the idea of social antagonism very well, but he was also influenced by Nietzsche, and the latter influence has produced elements of vitalism in Bataille's work. This is instructive because one of the most important features of theoretical vitalism is precisely its idea of the 'immanence' of one's own resources. In this sense, Nietzsche could be seen as an original thinker of sovereignty. Moreover, like Badiou, he can be described as an immanentist thinker.

All of this leads us to a resounding conclusion: *the people is sovereign*. We would even go further: without sovereignty – understood precisely as the singular indivisibility of power – there is no people (in the political sense). But here an important confusion may arise. When we say that 'the people are sovereign', if what we have in mind is the indivisibility of power and, in the same sense, the self-conferred prerogative of this people to take a decision vis-à-vis a social antagonism, it is evident that this is a general property of the people, which does not only apply to national peoples. This is a curious point, because if we use a more 'traditional' definition of the people, it may seem that there is a stronger connection between the two aspects. To clarify, then: we consider that there are several – perhaps infinite – forms of the sovereign people, and the geographical is only one of them. On the other hand, this conclusion obviously implies that the geographical form of the sovereign people is *also* valid. This is something that the contemporary left would not accept. It should be made clear that we are not arguing here that the nation is the only form of territorial unit that exists, has existed or can exist. It is obvious that it is not so. We merely wish to point out that when non-national territories are not present, at a given moment – in today's Europe, for example (since we do not believe that there exists any such a thing as a European identity) – they cannot simply be invented out of thin air.

As we have already pointed out, few contemporary intellectuals would accept these conclusions. Today's Marxists would resist them doggedly. The interesting thing is that these ideas do not necessarily have to be understood as anti-Marxist. The formulation of Marx and Engels, in the *Communist Manifesto*, is famous: 'The working men have no country'; on the other hand, we believe that no serious Marxist in history has believed that national politics can be ignored, so long as these nations exist. Lenin did not think that, nor Trotsky, nor, indeed, did Marx himself. The full quote from the *Manifesto* is as follows:

> The working men have no country. We cannot take from them what they have not got. Since the proletariat must first of all acquire political supremacy, must rise to be the leading class of the nation, must constitute itself *the* nation, it is, so far, itself national, though not in the bourgeois sense of the word.[8]

Gramsci, for his part, sums up this aspect very well: 'To be sure, the line of development is towards internationalism, but the point of departure is "national" – and it is from this point of departure that we must begin'.[9] Even in the more recent Marxist–Gramscian tradition, one finds thinkers who seem to have understood this idea well. Consider the following quote from Nicos Poulantzas:

> Only *a national transition to socialism* is possible: not in the sense of a universal model simply adapted to national particularities, but in the sense of a multiplicity of original roads to socialism, whose general principles, drawn from the theory and experience of the workers' movement, cannot be more than signs on the road.[10]

If it is true, then, that many contemporary Marxists would not accept this position, perhaps we would be better to consider them left-wing neoliberals.

In conclusion, we believe that the nation can perfectly well be seen as one of a series of possible populist antagonisms and, in the same sense, sovereign (as are all the others). Again, however, sovereignty in this sense can clearly only be an effect of a singular antagonism. This implies, once again, that sovereignty is incompatible with hegemonic logic. One could go further. Given that, as we have argued, the theory of hegemony is ultimately based on social plenitude, it is difficult to see how a hegemonic nationalism could avoid racism and social segregation, despite what defenders of this strategy, such as Iñigo Errejón, have said. The latter's lapidary comment on the matter was as follows: 'We must dispute the idea of Spain with the right'.[11] There are people on the left in Spain who would surely not accept Errejón's position, because they believe that it is impossible to separate the signifier 'Spain' from the conservative-Francoist right. To clarify, in this dispute, we are on the side of Errejón. On the other hand, if this strategy is based on hegemonic premises, we would have to align ourselves with those who would oppose it: there is no national plenitude – no matter how 'hegemonic' – that is not essentially fascist. Obviously, what we are not doing here is calling any defender of hegemony theory a racist. We are simply saying that this is a logical implication of such a theory, and if, in this context, an advocate of hegemony manages to avoid this implication, it is because they have abandoned de facto the premises of their own ideas. Before concluding, we believe it would be interesting to explore one last question – of a more political nature – that is directly related to all the conclusions we have set out so far and that has not yet been discussed. At the end of the first chapter, we conceded that the state can exist as a phantasy. If this is so, how can we explain the perspective on the state that occupies the minds of so many left-wing political activists? After all, these are people who have supposedly traversed this phantasy. This is a topic that clearly includes the issue of political parties. This, then, is where we will begin our final discussion, in the following chapter.

Notes

1 Alain Badiou, Pierre Bourdieu, Judith Butler, Georges Didi Huberman, Sadri Khiari and Jacques Rancière, *What Is a People?* (New York: Columbia University Press), 2013, pp. 22–23.
2 Alain Badiou, *Being and Event* (London: Continuum), 2005, p. 180.
3 Alain Badiou, *Ethics – An Essay on the Understanding of Evil* (London: Verso), 2001, p. 112.
4 Alain Badiou, Pierre Bourdieu, Judith Butler, Georges Didi Huberman, Sadri Khiari and Jacques Rancière, *What Is a People?* (New York: Columbia University Press), 2013, p. 30.
5 See: Timothy Appleton, *Escupir en la iglesia – Un sí de izquierdas al Brexit* (Madrid: Lengua de Trapo), 2020.
6 See: Dieter Grimm, *Sovereignty – The Origin and Future of a Political and Legal Concept* (New York: Columbia University Press), 2015.
7 Georges Bataille, *The Accursed Share – An Essay on General Economy* (New York: Zone Books), 1991, pp. 197–198.
8 Robert C. Tucker (Ed.), *The Marx-Engels Reader* (London: Norton), 1978, p. 488.
9 Antonio Gramsci, *Selections from the Prison Notebooks* (London: Lawrence and Wishart), 1998, p. 240.
10 Nicos Poulantzas, *State, Power, Socialism* (London: Verso), 2014, p. 118 (emphasis in the original).
11 https://ctxt.es/es/20181212/Politica/23449/%C3%AD%C3%B1igo-Errej%C3%B3n-entrevista-Comunidad-de-Madrid-pacto-Gabilondo-s%C3%ADmbolos-nacionales.htm.

Chapter 7

How should populists relate to political parties?

During the last era of triumphant neoliberalism – before the financial crisis of 2007–8 – many radical leftists had ceased to take part in established political parties, or indeed in political parties at all. Later, these same people went back to participating in such parties. Why this change? Apparently, leftist activists suddenly saw a possibility in political parties that they had previously ignored. Of what kind? The first question we must ask ourselves here is simple: what is the function of a political party? It seems clear that, in a 'democratic system' (which is in fact an oxymoron) a political party exists to win elections, especially general ones, in order to later be able to govern a state. It is equally clear that this is not compatible with the populist logic that we have outlined in this text, since it involves imposing an impossible unity on such a state, together with the social formation that accompanies it. We have already explained that this is the hegemonic myth, which we reject. Does this imply that populist politics must ignore the political parties that are essentially part of this state, *qua* hypothetical unity? Not necessarily. On the one hand, it is clear that populism does not have an *obligation* to participate in such parties – there are many radical groups that prefer not to; on the other hand, we do not consider it necessary to ignore political parties completely. Taking into account the difference between populism and 'state politics', then, why might it be in the interest of populists to join parties? One obvious explanation is that a mythical state – with its apparent vocation of social unification – does have material effects, which can affect the populist struggles one sometimes finds oneself involved in. It can be deduced that this is sometimes a more efficient way of militating. At what *level*, then, should populism participate in 'political parties'?

We have already stated that what unifies a socio-ontological situation is an imaginary. We have also argued that there exists more than one situation of this type. If so, it is logical that there also exists more than one imaginary. If it is considered, then, that the state represents the totality of a social order, all relevant struggles included, it would be logical to conclude that the state represents, for many people, the *imaginary of imaginaries*. If this idea is accepted, we can infer that an oppositional political party – which claims to fight against such a figure – would represent *an imaginary version of the people themselves*. In other words, if imaginaries can

DOI: 10.4324/9781003431916-10

in turn have an imaginary form, the people can also have one (in the form of a party). It must be reiterated that we are only talking, here, about a mythical state. We are not reproducing the argument, with which we do not logically agree, of Laclau and Mouffe, that the people can oppose a social order and represent it at the same time. We are simply arguing that it is possible – from the perspective of a people – to maintain the phantasy of a more general change in the system of social relations. Another obvious implication of this argument is that the imaginary form of the people does not correspond with a *real* people. So, what form would the people assume in this second sense? We would say that the real people is that which is capable of manifesting its oppositional-antagonistic dimension at all times. It could also incorporate its plural dimension, although this is not necessarily the case. How, then, are the imaginary form of the people and its real form related? Simply put, the real version must *invade* the imaginary version. This reflects the way in which the 'destiny' of the real – according to Lacanian theory – partly involves invading and destabilising an imaginary. In other words, a process must take place by which the political party – as an imaginary people (since it is supposed to refer to a total state) – is forced to open up to the people as such. What would such a process look like? On this occasion, we are going to consider an empirical example.

I am now going to talk about the Labour Party in Great Britain, an example I know rather well. The Labour Party is one of the official parties of the supposed totality of the British state. It even has the status of 'official opposition'. This is partly because it doesn't usually win elections (which might be an eye-opening fact in itself!) Now, in 2015, this party elected a populist leader, Jeremy Corbyn. Corbyn can be considered a populist since he participates in various political struggles of very different characters, while always emphasising their antagonistic dimension. The rise of Corbyn precipitated one of the most important crises in the history of the Labour Party. A year after his victory, the Labour group in parliament passed an unprecedented motion of no confidence against its own leader, and almost all members of the shadow cabinet resigned at once; some also campaigned unofficially against their party leader (not to mention, on occasion, their own party) in subsequent elections; others resigned from the party altogether; and over the next three years there was a split in the party, thus creating a new party in the British parliament. Did the fact that Corbyn was a populist, in our terms, really affect the 'statist desire' (which is unified and unifying, the imaginary of imaginaries) that had traditionally run through this party?

In itself, the rise of Corbyn did not imply a great change in the mentality of the Labour Party; on the other hand, a very interesting process occurred in parallel, which concerned a new group, *Momentum*, that was created to support Corbyn, and whose very name referred to his candidacy to be party leader. First of all, this group tried to force open – in the name of Corbyn – the Labour Party itself, to the popular demands that constitutively existed outside the party. We are referring above all to the way in which *Momentum* was, on the one hand, just another faction within the Labour Party – thus participating in its imaginary aspect – while, on the other, it was open to people who were not members of the party. Hence the nervous breakdown that this group brought about among the Labour MPs in Parliament: they saw that the corporatist unity they supported was being put at risk. For example, the Deputy Leader of the party (Tom Watson) described *Momentum* as 'a rabble'; another of the most famous Labour MPs accused it of being an anti-Semitic group (despite the fact that its leader and founder is Jewish); many more said they were Trotskyists and should be expelled from the party.[1] The Tories even entered the debate (perhaps to support their corporatist counterparts in the Labour Party). The Conservative government's Chancellor of the Exchequer incoherently described *Momentum*, in a speech at the House of Commons, as 'a neo-fascist group'.[2]

A symptomatic effect of all this was the fact that in his first interviews with the BBC and other outlets, Corbyn's number two, John McDonnell, was asked again and again whether he was more committed to extra-parliamentary or parliamentary political action.[3] For a long time, British journalists obsessed over this topic. All of which shows the threat that the early *Momentum* – which was an ally of McDonnell – posed to the British 'body politic'. Another symptom was that the right of the Labour Party – those who are allies of the former right-wing leader Tony Blair – founded a counter-movement, which was called 'Clause One', in reference to the first clause of the Labour Party constitution, which states that Labour must organise a group *in* the British Parliament. This was an implicit rebuke to *Momentum*'s 'extra-parliamentary' strategy. It could be added that all these moments cropped up almost automatically in this period, which shows that in a way everyone understood very well what was at stake. Finally, and partly as a result of all this pressure, *Momentum* closed its doors to people who were not members of the Labour Party, citing the question of party discipline – the party was supposedly unable to take responsibility for non-members – and the project ended, thus falling into incoherence and irrelevance. Nevertheless, its first phase was glorious and very important. Perhaps it could have continued as a bridge between the two different understandings of politics, but the 'unifying' pressure of the establishment proved unbearable to it.

Again, aren't we very close, here, to the theory of hegemony? When we talk about the occupation of an imaginary people by heterogeneous demands, are we not arguing the same as Laclau and Mouffe? We believe not, because, once again, we do not see any transference between these struggles. This means that we do not have to choose between them, or rank them, in order to 'take power'. This is precisely because for us, the idea that there is a finite social space, in which such phenomena might take place, is false. In fact, the highest point of hegemonic theory, in this area, is Laclau's conclusion, which we mentioned in Chapter 1: that all politics is representative. What we have wanted to portray here is a more complex dialectic: that the fundamentally presentative character of politics (to put it in terms of Rancière's 'populism') can sometimes be expressed – albeit indirectly – within a system that claims to be purely representative. Thus, we end up in a situation in which the absolute heterogeneity of the people can be effectively opposed to the One of the state, *qua* state of states. Those who think that these issues are merely a matter of current political trends should probably keep in mind that what we are dealing with here is in fact a quite traditional problem for the left, running at least from Lenin's book *State and Revolution* to the Chinese Cultural Revolution, which was an attempt – partly under Mao's orders – to revolutionise the Chinese Communist Party itself, plus the state it had created, from within.

Notes

1 www.bbc.com/news/uk-politics-35009342; www.youtube.com/watch?v=n_FXpemQ9vM; www.telegraph.co.uk/politics/2019/12/13/jeremy-corbyns-momentum-cult-must-kicked-labour-says-former/.
2 www.independent.co.uk/news/uk/politics/sajid-javid-momentum-neo-facist-labour-party-antisemitisim-jewish-a8280601.html.
3 For example: www.telegraph.co.uk/news/politics/Jeremy_Corbyn/11893986/Jeremy-Cor byns-top-team-encouraged-street-riots.html; www.telegraph.co.uk/comment/telegraph-view/ 11893307/The-disturbing-roots-of-Corbynism-exposed.html; www.theguardian.com/com mentisfree/2016/aug/05/corbyn-cant-dismiss-mps-brexit-centre-stage; www.newstatesman. com/politics/economy/2018/09/who-real-john-mcdonnell; www.voanews.com/europe/brexit-brings-about-political-role-reversal.

Chapter 8

Conclusion

Future politics

In the first chapter of this book, we concluded that populism is the only political form that is capable of emptying out all social ontology. Then, we discovered that this form should be considered left-wing, although we added the possibility of its perversion, in simulacrous form. Next, we argued that the necessary mark of a populist politics is popular enthusiasm, which we associated with a register of *jouissance* that is irreducible to hegemonic processes. We also explained that the production that emerges from this experience can be considered true, which imposes an ethical responsibility on the subject that has constructed it: to persevere in their project of being. We subsequently defined a populist leader as someone who is able to publicly display such an ethical characteristic, thus allowing others to identify with their example. Next, we looked at the question of nationalism, which has so often been associated with populism. We argued that the people is sovereign, in the sense that their powers of political decision are indivisible, but we explained that this is not an exclusive trait of the national people. However, we added that national peoples *also* show this characteristic, despite the prejudices of certain representatives of what we (ironically) called the neoliberal left. Finally, we argued that populists have the option of participating in the political parties that represent the state *qua* imaginary of imaginaries, but only from outside and, once again, antagonistically. After setting out all of these positions, we consider that we have provided the necessary foundations for a renewed thinking of political populism. Should we be more explicit about the concrete political implications of this theory? We feel that in a theoretical work, it is not urgent to be so explicit. Furthermore, as far as populist theory is concerned, it would be inappropriate to attempt it, since populism precisely depends on action by the people, not by intellectuals. However, it would perhaps be possible to amplify, before finishing, a couple of practical implications of our theory, which have come up in passing in this book.

We have explained that our approach thinks the coexistence of singular political struggles. This means that at the political level, we are allowed to unconditionally embrace each of them, if we wish to do so. Examples that could be included are: the economic struggle, the struggle against racism, the feminist struggle, the struggle against homophobia, defence of trans people, defence of animals, environmentalism, etc. To be clear, we consider the groups that are associated with each of these

DOI: 10.4324/9781003431916-11

struggles to be examples of *a people*. It might be added that this list represents well-known examples, but surely there are more, and it cannot be ruled out that even more will emerge in the future. Are some more 'important' than others? Perhaps it can be argued that certain antagonisms have more implications at the level of everyday life, but this consideration is irrelevant. As we do not believe that there can be a panoptical perspective upon them, we will not search for criteria by which to compare them. And, most importantly of all: the subjective aspect is decisive here. It is even possible that one person – who can participate in more than one subjectivity at the same time – will find themselves on the 'popular' side of certain struggles and not of others. Or even that they disagree that some of them even exist. Once again, at the theoretical level it matters not. The point is simply that it is not necessary to choose between them at a mythical social level. We believe that a key effect of all this is that it frees us from the endless debates about which of the struggles has priority. Hegemonists are used to saying that such debates are the product of a Marxist epistemological error, of wanting to reduce every political antagonism to the struggle between social classes. In reality, however, we believe that they end up falling into the same trap, by insisting on a condensation of struggles, regardless of the uncertainty over who is going to occupy the central position in such a condensation.

Another important connotation of our theory is that populism must be blatantly antagonistic to the status quo. Many are scared by this aspect. To them, it sounds like pistols. It might be added that this reticence extends to intellectuals. The number of academic debates on populism that we have witnessed in recent times in which the participants want to study the subject in detail precisely in order subsequently to be able to limit it, or even to eliminate it from the world, is incredible. Moreover, we have even seen that defenders of hegemony often come to the same conclusion. This is strange because hegemony is supposedly also based on antagonism. However, it seems unable to assume its own premise, in this respect. Why? As we already explained, we consider that hegemony substantialises the social space in which an antagonism can arise, thus making the latter into a confrontation between two opponents that are equally substantial and, in the same way, mutually recognisable. It seems clear to us that this can produce a fight to the death. We have also explained that our response to this conclusion is based on a decentring of the social order, which de-balances the relevant antagonisms, thus completely depriving them of their potential for blind violence. We would conclude, then, that this movement is what allows us to embrace antagonism in all its radicality. Another name for this radicality is singularity, and we consider that one effect of this singularity is that it allows antagonism not to lose sight of its universalist vocation, since a singularity is not associated with any particular rank in a pre-established social order. In other words, no person should be excluded *a priori* from its horizon of action. If it were, it would have become a simulacrum.

There are further political implications of our abandonment of social plenitude. For example, for us it is never valid to attempt to 'rule', 'govern', 'take command', much less 'take power', within a certain social order. If we did this, the kind of politics we are proposing would abolish itself at the very moment of its consummation. One consequence of this is that – as Jorge Alemán once commented – 'the state always belongs to others',[1] and this conclusion includes the political parties associated with it. That is, we see political parties simply as a vehicle to achieving a different political goal: they are never a political end in themselves and should at all times be treated with appropriate scepticism and caution. Our rejection of social plenitude also involves never trying to create 'a new common sense', to use the Gramscian revisionist platitude. It is evident that we have reached this conclusion because for us there is no terrain in which this could be possible, except imaginarily, and this aspect seems to us to be simply dangerous. In the same way, at no point should we populists think in terms of social pacification or rationalisation, nor of creating a better 'society' or 'world'. We do not consider these to be legitimate goals for an emancipatory politics. Ours is simply a call to justice, which produces a political struggle, in a very specific situation, and we consider its 'global consequences' to be utterly imponderable. In reaching the preceding conclusion, we are not trying to say that new social orders or a new common sense will not appear to be created; we are simply saying that if this happens, it will be not as a direct but rather as an indirect effect of our militancy, for the simple reason that such goals do not constitute our objects (*a*). We believe it is important not to confuse these two aspects.

I would like to add one last word. When one advocates populism, it often elicits a similar reaction: 'You have too romantic a view of the people. What happens, for example, when the people make a mistake? In fact, now that we're on the subject, has the people ever been right about anything?' There is a quote from Badiou in answer to this point that I really like. Near the end of his early Maoist text, *Theory of the Subject*, Badiou states: 'As far as I am concerned, I have confidence in the people and in the working class in direct proportion to my lack of belief in them.'[2] In other words, it makes no sense to have an abstract faith in the people (although in truth, populism was never about that); on the other hand, if we do not have confidence in what – sometimes – a people can do, emancipation would be stillborn. Or worse, it would be born alive but unable to grow, or produce anything, except more deaths. We believe that this idea is in itself a good justification for the theoretical program that we have begun to outline in this book. That is to say, if the left decides to abandon populism, the only thing that will happen is that the right will produce a simulacrous version of it. And it will succeed (because in truth, its task is always easier). It can even be said that this is already happening in our countries. Let's hope it's not too late to stop it.

Notes

1 www.youtube.com/watch?v=iVTBd_jytyY&feature=youtu.be&fbclid=IwAR0KRH-dMI05PTGhjT3fXKEFwbeInPV8p3o-oRomyk0qiqtoRSxnvQvkQVA.
2 Alain Badiou, *Theory of the Subject* (London: Continuum), 2013, p. 322.

A few short essays on political matters

Chapter 1

What is 'the populism of singularities'?

The virulence of some of the recent debates between so-called *TERFs* and *trans-feminists* – particularly on Twitter, which increasingly resembles a Hobbesian state of nature – might cause one to look with nostalgia upon the debates between the 'economists' and revolutionaries during the Second International, which merely resulted in the First World War. A further example of this type of dispute within the left over the priority of demands is set out in the bestselling Spanish book *La trampa de la diversidad*, by Daniel Bernabé. In this text, Bernabé argues that all the different forms of political battles that the left engages in must ultimately be referred to that surrounding the economy. Are such fights to the death for pure prestige really necessary, between people who consider themselves to be on the left? Are we condemned to disagree violently, while the right steals our clothes at night? Perhaps it depends on the theory that one uses to think about politics, and this is one of the reasons why I have written my latest book: *La política que viene*.[1] What argument do I set out therein?

The fundamental wager of *La política que viene* is as follows: although (left) populism continues to be the best way to think about politics, its theoretical bases must be reconsidered. How so? Populism has been seen for a long time – especially by those who follow the work of outstanding Argentine political theorist Ernesto Laclau – as a synonym of hegemony. The Spanish politician Íñigo Errejón has made a good ventriloquism of Laclau's position, saying:

> populist discourse is that which unifies highly diverse positions and social sectors in a dichotomization of the political field that opposes the traditional elites to the 'people' *qua* construction, through which the subaltern sectors successfully demand the representation of a forgotten or betrayed general interest.

In other words, if their cause is generalised, the people have the possibility of leading – of 'hegemonising', in the etymological sense – the social field from which they had previously found themselves excluded. The argument I make in my book is that it is impossible for this formulation to be correct. Why?

First, I believe that 'the people' should be considered a singularity. What does this mean? It means that we are dealing with an element that militates from the

DOI: 10.4324/9781003431916-13

perspective of the void of a social situation. That is to say, the populist subject is that which comes to deconstruct a social system. In fact, Errejón captured this idea well when he used the word 'subaltern'. Thus, if the term hegemony – which Errejón himself fully embraces – refers to the leadership of a given social field, we should understand it as cleaving to the fullness, rather than the emptiness, of such a field. This in fact makes it the opposite of the people. Another way of summarizing this would be to say that hegemony is associated with the authorities and the people is what comes to oppose them. From my perspective, there can never be a transference between the two.

It seems unlikely that defenders of the identification between populism and hegemony, such as Errejón, have made a theoretical error as basic as that of confusing the emptiness of a society with its plenitude. One must therefore concede that the theoretical picture they present is actually more complex. What Laclau, for his part, has argued is that the political antagonism between the people and the elite must not only be considered 'the limit of any social objectivity whatsoever' (to use his own phrase), but also represent the particular demands that can be found within this same objectivity. He will add that hegemony is the name of the 'articulation' between these two aspects. In other words, Laclau believes that hegemony condenses the antagonisms that are internal to a society, thus referring them to the ultimate antagonism (which in turn metonymises the void) of the same order.

However, this logic – as sophisticated as it may seem – is equally unacceptable. One cannot have certain antagonisms existing within others, because this would also imply that there can be 'a limit of any social objectivity whatsoever' within another, which would be logically absurd. How do I propose to resolve these contradictions? The answer I give in my book is surprisingly simple, even if its implications are not. I argue that there are as many social orders as there are antagonisms, and that no 'meta-order' can be expected to unify all of them. I believe that in this way the singularity of a people can be preserved. This is what I call 'the populism of singularities'.

Here I should like to mention another important theme that emerges from Laclau's work: that of 'the impossibility of society'. I consider that the populism of singularities refines, or even completes, this idea. Laclau saw this impossibility as the result of a contingent – and multivariant – division between the people and the elite. What I propose, more radically, is that society is impossible not because of this, but because it in fact presents a pure dispersion, of the infinite antagonisms – each subtracted from a different order of being – that we experience as humans. This last term – 'humans' – does not imply a return to what I take to be the prehistory of social theory, i.e. classical humanism. It simply confirms that the scale on which we must now think about politics is not that of a society (which is impossible) but that of an individual, who is embedded in different fields of being, as well as in the antagonistic dramas contained within each of the latter.

My theoretical conclusions at this level have in part been inspired by the philosophical 'new realism' proposed by authors such as the young German thinker Markus Gabriel, who argues that the world, on the Heideggerian definition – that is, as domain of domains – does not exist. In saying this, Gabriel does not mean that the domains that this world is supposed to incorporate do not exist, but rather that the very fact that these domains do exist is incompatible with their condensation within an all-encompassing world. Gabriel speaks of the 'world' because he is a philosopher. Since I am a political theorist, I prefer to speak about society. In the same way, then, that Gabriel concludes that the world does not exist, I would say, paraphrasing Margaret Thatcher (albeit with a different political implication), that society does not exist. With this we can go back to the debates between, for example, the TERFs and the transfeminists.

According to the premises of the 'populism of singularities', the tensions between different political struggles – antagonisms – would be resolved at the subjective level and not within philosophy, which implies that at no time can we, nor indeed do we have to, choose between such demands at the collective level. In fact, the observation that a person can perfectly well be, for example, a feminist and not support the trans demand at the same time hardly seems surprising. Everything will depend on one's personal interpellations. And there exists no 'ontological' tribunal that might choose between the relevant positions. I believe that this point is crucial at the political level, because it serves to 'relativise' the distinctions between such positions.

A more recognised example, perhaps, is that which I referred to earlier. Someone (Bernabé, for example) might argue that the economic struggle is decisive in politics. Indeed, many Marxists have done so for a very long time. Sometimes one feels that such people are like spies, looking for traces of the economy behind movements such as feminism, environmentalism or gay pride. This search reminds me of the paranoia of the ideologues during the first phase of Francoism, who used to argue that behind Republicanism there was Bolshevism, behind Bolshevism there was Judaism, behind Judaism there was Islam and behind Islam there was Africanism. Now, although it is evident that one could legitimately defend that the economic struggle has more implications in individuals' daily lives than other political forms, we should not deduce from this that that kind of antagonism has an 'ontological' privilege. Once again, to militate or not in this regard will be a 'personal' decision, which will depend on the balance of the situations (of being) in which an individual finds themselves. This also implies that disputes between, for example, 'communists' and 'populists' (here understood as ontological pluralists) make little sense.

Now, hegemonists will say that hegemony has an important advantage compared to traditional Marxism, namely that hegemony is able to mediate between the struggle for political power in general and the plurality of antagonisms. But this idea seems, frankly, to be a sophism. In Laclau's work, hegemonic condensation is an ontological, not an ontic, principle, so there is really no possible mediation between the two moments: hegemony necessarily suffocates its opposition, wherever it comes from. I must confess that I never quite understood the difference between Laclau and Lenin, at this level. If Lenin believes in hegemony, and so does Laclau, and if, moreover, the relevant scale of hegemony is a given social order, what difference does it make if this leadership is seen as teleological (which is the accusation that Laclau launched against Leninism) or not? What does it matter if the Marxist 'laws of history' are suspended or not? I suppose that this could be considered an interesting distinction at the theoretical level, but its political implications seem to me to be nil. Furthermore, hegemony does not rule out, as its advocates often claim, a total (Leninist) revolution. We just don't know what exact shape it would have. But this would be decided by the relevant order, not by a few theorists of hegemony.

Having presented the keys to our conceptualisation, the following question can probably be guessed: what happens at the state level? That is, if we abandon the hegemonic struggle, would this not represent another iteration of an impotent anarchist logic? Isn't the populism of singularities just another theoretical justification for heresy? Not necessarily. This theory implies nothing more nor less than that there is no ultimate social horizon within which the competition between the various struggles that might arise could be adjudicated. For example, it does not rule out populists working with the political parties of what is usually called the state (which also does not truly exist, since the society on which it is supposed to be based does not exist either). It only implies that our struggles do not ultimately coincide with the aims of these parties, and they never will. In the words of another important Argentinian populist theorist, Jorge Alemán, 'the state always belongs to others'.

In conclusion, I hope that the argument I present in my book – especially its central conceptual element, the populism of singularities – can contribute to a new phase of left-wing political militancy, in which the 'philosophical' tensions between the various ways in which this militancy is expressed will be considered irrelevant. I personally believe that this type of disarmament is very urgent and necessary, due to the 'surplus value' it accrues to the radical right, which is always the shadow that comes to engulf the light produced by true populism, by which I mean, of course, that of the left.

Note

1 Timothy Appleton, *La política que viene – Hacia un populismo de las singularidades* (Barcelona: NED Editions), 2022. The present text – which was partly intended to summarise the central thesis of the above book – is an English translation of an article published in the Spanish newspaper *El Salto*, on 3 May 2022.

Chapter 2

Was will das Volk?

'We cannot shut out the scream of Reich: the masses were not deceived; at a particular time, they actually wanted a fascist regime!'[1] The tone of this remark by Deleuze, which is abstracted from a conversation he had with Foucault in 1972, evokes the bewilderment one finds in Freud's classic question, cited in Jones' celebrated biography: '*Was will das Weib?*' (What does woman want/desire?). Combining the two locutions, one could formulate the question of the day as follows: *Was will das Volk?* (What does the people want/desire?) Why do I consider this an urgent question? I speak from a geographically European perspective, above all, that of my adopted country, Spain. Ten years after the 'Spanish Spring' – 15M – it seems we are experiencing a kind of political Autumn: the hope that emerged from that magical moment in 2011 seems now to have dissipated, especially following the victory of the right in the recent elections in Madrid. As is often the case, the disorientation of the left that has set in during the last few years has highlighted certain theoretical questions, of the kind raised by Deleuze: What if the masses are not, as we sometimes tend to think, the privileged agent of emancipation, but are in fact the opposite? Or, to put it in our usual vocabulary: is 'the people' left- or right-wing (if we assume that the left can be directly associated with emancipation)? Logically, there are three possible answers to this question: i) the people can either be left-wing *or* right-wing; ii) the people is right-wing; iii) the people is left-wing. In this short essay, I shall consider these answers one by one. I will conclude that the third answer is the correct one, although I will add an important caveat.

The people can be either right- or left-wing

The idea that the people can be either right- or left-wing is defended by Ernesto Laclau and Chantal Mouffe, among others. The criterion they introduce is derived from their reading of Gramsci. It has to do with Gramsci's principle of 'transformism' (or 'passive revolution'). *Transformism* describes the moment when an 'organic crisis' (to use another term from the same author) in a social system resolves itself in a conservative rather than a 'progressive' direction. What's the difference between these two possibilities? A transformist resolution of a social crisis would be when the relevant society manages to consolidate itself. Hence the reason I am

DOI: 10.4324/9781003431916-14

calling it conservative: it *conserves* the existing society. A progressive solution, on the other hand, would imply that the previous system predominantly changes into another. From Gramsci's traditionally Marxist viewpoint, this change will involve the proletariat becoming the ruling class, thus displacing the previous ruling class, the bourgeoisie. Laclau and Mouffe, for their part, would not accept this characteristic, since they do not believe that the proletariat possesses a historical destiny in this sense. On the other hand, they do argue that there exist different hegemonic axes, and when one of these manages to displace another, then we find ourselves in a 'progressive' moment. In the first case – that of a net social consolidation – Laclau and Mouffe would say that we are dealing with a right-wing hegemony, and in the second – a net social reorganisation – with a left-wing hegemony. Moreover, since they believe that the privileged agent of a hegemony is 'the people', it is now possible to understand how they might conclude that a people – plus its 'philosophical ideology' of populism – may be either right- or left-wing. Does this conclusion make sense? I think it is undermined by what I would call *the aporia of hegemony*. This is a complex issue that I shall briefly try to explain. It has to do with the status of the category of antagonism in the theory of Laclau and Mouffe.

I believe that 'the aporia of hegemony' is essentially a mathematical problem. It seems to me that it is never clear – not even, in truth, to Laclau and Mouffe themselves – whether antagonism – which according to them is the fundamental ontological aspect of populism (i.e., of politics as such) – should be considered a *singular* or a *plural* phenomenon. In other words, is antagonism, on the one hand, the unique limit of a 'social system' or is it, in contrast, something that appears multiple times within such a system? These authors would certainly answer that it is both things at once, and furthermore that the short-circuit between a particular antagonism – one among others – and a universal antagonism – which limits the social field in which the former can be found – constitutes a very precise definition of the hegemonic process (this is the essence of Laclau's argument about empty signifiers). I would argue, however, that this position is illogical. An antagonism cannot be both the limit of any social objectivity whatsoever and something that is simultaneously scattered around within that same objectivity. There cannot be 'limits of all social objectivity' within other 'limits of all social objectivity'. This problem evokes the Russell paradox, since it implies that antagonism simultaneously is and is not the condition of possibility of a social whole. It is a difficult paradox, on which I hope to publish more very soon. It is relevant here because Laclau and Mouffe's argument about the ambiguous political status of populism is based on aggregations between the plurality of antagonisms that supposedly exist within a social order. If it is true, however, that what is at stake is antagonisms in the plural, then the *singular* aspect of antagonism – *qua* limit of a social order – inevitably fades away (precisely because it is incompatible with its plural dimension). If this is the case, however, then the relevant social whole automatically becomes intensional, i.e. a replete totality. The effect of this is inevitable: every attempt at hegemony is aimed towards a social plenitude. But this would imply that such a project is by definition an attempt at consolidation, i.e. it is transformist. Thus we come to our second option: the people is (necessarily) right-wing. To further develop this idea, I think it is useful to pass from Laclau and Mouffe to another post-Althusserian thinker, Alain Badiou.

The people is right-wing

What Badiou calls the *subject* is something that adheres to the void of what he dubs a *situation*. This is why Badiou argues that an 'evental site' – upon which there may later be built an event, which is precisely what breaks with a situation, thus producing a political antagonism – is, as he says, 'on the edge of the void'. For the same reason, he considers that an evental site constitutes a singularity (i.e. an element that belongs to a set without being included in it). I would say that the same logic can be applied to what we are calling a people. If we assume that the subject of politics, in Badiou's sense, is a people, it can be asserted that the latter adheres to the void point of a social order, thus producing a singular antagonism between the people and the elite. This conclusion is important in part because it offers to resolve the aporia of hegemony that I described earlier. That is, if we accept Badiou's logic, we can conclude that any true antagonism is singular, rather than plural. Later on, Badiou adds another point to his theory, which is especially important to us in this essay. He presents this point in his book *Ethics*.

In the above text, Badiou argues that if a subject of politics, after it is born (because before the event, such a subject does not exist), adheres to the *plenitude* of a situation, rather than to its void, then we are encountering one of the main ways of abandoning, or suffocating, the event with which it is associated. This is not a simple process, because when it has already been subtracted from a situation, an event cannot simply be ignored; it must be violently rejected. In these circumstances, something that looks like an event is produced, although it is in fact what Badiou calls a *simulacrum*. The paradigm of the simulacrum, for Badiou, is Nazism. This is because Badiou considers it to be a bad copy of his favourite example of a political event: the Russian Revolution. This last idea might remind us of the apocryphal comment by the German philosopher Walter Benjamin, that every fascist outbreak bears witness to a failed revolution. Or it could be seen as a variation on the idea of Marx that history occurs twice: first as tragedy, then as farce. One can see how Badiou's argument fits with our previous conclusion about the theory of hegemony, i.e. that the latter it necessarily right-wing, since, having glimpsed the contingency of a social situation, it subsequently dedicates itself to covering up this contingency. Once again, it can be concluded that populism *qua* hegemony is necessarily right-wing. If this is the case, however, how do we get to our third option: that the people is (necessarily) left-wing? Badiou has already given us an important clue. To explain it fully, however, I think it would first be useful to consider the argument of the paradigmatic representative of this idea; I have in mind the work of Jorge Alemán.

The people is left-wing

Alemán has long insisted that populism should not be considered right-wing, but specifically left-wing. Why? Like Badiou, he believes that political emancipation is defined by adhering to the singular void point of a social situation. Alemán coins the term *Soledad: Común* (Common: Solitude) to refer to this phenomenon. This term nicely captures the dimensions of singularity (Solitude) and universality (Common) that any genuinely emancipatory politics must incorporate, if one takes into account that this singularity is precisely what precipitates an antagonism that is capable of appealing to *everyone* within a specific situation. For Alemán, to be in favour of this singularity is to be on the left. If there is a theoretical parallel between Alemán and Badiou at this level, however, why haven't we simply cited Badiou's theory and left the matter there? We have not done so because there is an important difference between the two thinkers. Badiou – like another important Lacanian, Slavoj Žižek – has dubbed the privileged subject of a singular emancipation 'the proletariat'. As we have said, Alemán, in contrast, calls it the people and goes on to defend 'populism' as against the 'communism' of Badiou (or Žižek). I believe that this distinction is decisive because I feel that it would be difficult to defend the true singularity of a political sequence if this very singularity is 'overdetermined' by a (capitalist) social ontology of the type required by the projects of Badiou and Žižek. In truth, I think that the position of Badiou and Žižek leads us back to the aporia of hegemony. Although both of them would reject the latter term, the aporia implies that the social is excessive with respect to an antagonism, and I feel that this is precisely what Badiou and Žižek end up defending. This, then, is the mistake that I think Alemán manages to avoid. In this sense, the use of the dual terms populism and the people in his work is not simply a matter of political taste; it goes to the very heart of ontology. For the same reason, this third position – that of Alemán – is the one that seems to me to be the most logical of all. Thus we can conclude, with Alemán, that the people is necessarily left-wing. But that is not the end of the story. To complete it, we must return to Badiou.

When liberal European journalists curse the name of populism, associating it with the racist right, this is not, as Wittgenstein might have said, 'a stupid prejudice'. It is true that racist populism has a certain connection with true populism, which, as we have said, must be considered left-wing. What does this connection consist of? What they have in common is that they are both based on a real ontological difference: a singular antagonism. On the other hand, as we have explained, they have two very different ways of dealing with this difference. The right tries to violently shut it down, while the left tries to make it even more visible, in order to try to create something new within the ambit of a situation, a creation that will involve a different kind of violence. Following the same logic, I believe that even though populism as such must indeed be considered left-wing, such populism can in fact be perverted, thus producing a secondary and fake version of it. In this sense, I would propose, following Badiou, that we call right-wing populism a *simulacrum* of populism. Once again, a key aspect of this phenomenon is *chronology*. Recently, we have seen numerous examples: for example, *Vox* occupying the space that was established (and then abandoned?) by *Podemos* in Spain, Trump walking through the door that Bernie Sanders had opened in the U.S., Bolsonaro (albeit temporarily) replacing Lula and Rousseff in Brazil, even the way (little known outside of Britain, apparently) in which the British right colonised the demand to leave the European Union, which was once a key proposal of the British left.

Conclusion

In conclusion, the people is essentially left-wing, although there is the possibility that it will subsequently be perverted, thus producing a simulacrum of itself. One – probably more controversial – deduction that can be made from this conclusion is that we must run the risk of the simulacrum of emancipation if we want to experience emancipation in the first place. Many will see this as a dangerous opinion. I think they are wrong. After all, what genuinely democratic process is risk-free? Also, what would the alternative be? To make our peace with what already exists? This is not an option that I feel we should consent to. In sum, I believe that those of us who consider ourselves to be on the radical left must continue to wager on 'the people', even if we run the risk of opening the door to its perversion by the radical right. To put it in the words of Badiou himself: '*Mieuz vaut un désastre qu'un désêtre*'.

Note

1   This article was published in the magazine *#lacanemancipa: The Magazine of the Lacanian Left* on 13 July 2021.

Chapter 3

Beyond the empty signifier
Lalangue and *Black Lives Matter*

The political movement that has grown out of the tragic murder of George Floyd has produced debates of all kinds, all over the world.[1] However, we feel it is pertinent for us to discuss details of language and political subjectivity that are not usually analysed in other contexts. A good example of this is the current slogan of the group that leads (although one should also ask the question of what it means to 'lead', in this context) the American mobilisations, Black Lives Matter. Its current slogan is: 'Defund the police!' We consider that this is a key element of the movement's discourse, but we also note that no serious theoretical analysis of the phrase has yet been carried out. So, what does this phrase mean? How can we account for its connotations and repercussions at a political level?

Defund is a modern word – contemporary, in fact – a neologism, of obscure origin. 'To fund', in English, has a connotation of social/civic generosity. In the same vein, 'Defund' is a word that seems to be deliberately provocative: resentful, some conservatives would say, as if it constituted a direct negation of the total social good. What interests us most about the negative prefix, however, is that it has two different interpretations, which are not present in its positive form. On the one hand, it could connote diverting funds from the police (an increasingly militarised force, which has even more resources than the United States Army itself, in the latter's foreign adventures) towards other forms of social work. Its other possible meaning implies directly abolishing the police force. Perhaps by pointing out these elements, the crux of the phrase can already be glimpsed. To put it in traditional terms, we have, on the one hand, the existence of a 'reformist' demand, on the other a 'revolutionary' demand. In this sense, it is a signifier that is neither revolutionary nor reformist, but *both at the same time*. In other words, the prefix introduces a radical undecidability in the relevant discourse, which – at the very moment it is put into circulation as a political signifier – makes a subsequent political decision even more peremptory. It is as if it were a phrase that requires constant explanation. At the same time, it oscillates between two different modes of *jouissance* (to put it in psychoanalytic terms). In a word, the very enunciation of the phrase produces a dilemma, thus opening up a whole field of possible political militancy. Let's give a couple of examples of the political effects the phrase has had.

DOI: 10.4324/9781003431916-15

It is very interesting to note what happened in the demonstration on 8 June, with the mayor of Minneapolis, the state in which George Floyd died, an event that precipitated the entire wave of protests. The mayor – Jacob Frey – can be considered a true progressive, a political representative who is genuinely leftist, and was basically on the side of the protesters. For instance, it is very rare for an official political representative to attend such a demonstration. That is why it is even more interesting to note that the protesters kicked him out of the event. What occurred exactly? Once again, Mayor Frey began his speech by expressing sympathy for the protesters. Laying out his position, he said that racism has to stop. He even went further. He made a structural analysis of the problem, stating that racism exists even where it is not directly perceived and for this reason, a great radical intervention was required in the institutions of civil society. We find nothing to criticise here. What we find interesting, however, is that on this occasion, not even the typical structural criticism of the contemporary left was considered adequate to the situation. At one point, Frey was interrupted by an organiser who addressed him directly, saying: 'We don't care what you say. We only have one question for you, and we want you to answer yes or no: "Are you in favour of defunding the police or not?"' Of course, it was very difficult – almost impossible – for this career politician to answer the question directly. You can almost see his 'existential crisis' unfolding in real time, in the video of the meeting. In the end, Frey answers: 'No'. We can assume that if he had not given this answer, he could not have continued as mayor. Perhaps the best that can be said about him is that at least he did not try to avoid the question, which is what many politicians would have done. But from the point of view of the protesters, of course, in that moment he displayed his bad faith, and he had to withdraw from the demonstration, to a chorus of jeers.

Another example we consider interesting is that of Kamala Harris, who is currently vice-president of the United States but who at the time of the protests was simply a female black senator who had participated in the Democratic Party primaries as a possible candidate for the presidency of the country. Harris can be located on the right-wing of the Democratic Party, has previously been a Detroit Attorney and was reputed to be an exceptionally draconian functionary. Nevertheless, she was forced, around the time of the protests, on one of America's most popular television shows, *The View*, to defend the demand to defund the police without hesitation. It was a moment of high drama. The interesting thing about the situation was that Harris found herself obliged to defend the slogan in all its radicality, because in such a context (one of enemy ideological fire), it was impossible to distinguish the revolutionary demand from the reformist one without abandoning the defence of the movement as a whole. One interesting aspect here is that it shows how a truly popular demand breaks with any left or right schema, thus undermining established political structures. So, how should we analyse the phrase 'Defund the police!' theoretically?

Many would surely say that this is an example of what in theory is called an *empty signifier*, in the sense of a signifier without a fixed signified, thus allowing people to project different signifieds onto it. It must be added that the empty signifier, at least according to Laclau's theory of the term, also contains a moment of ambiguity. It implies a short-circuit between what Laclau calls 'the universal' and 'the particular'. Where might these two aspects be found in the Black Lives Matter movement? First, the universalist dimension can be found in the demand to abolish the police. Some would call this aspect 'utopian' (they have done so). Of course, Laclau would not have used this word to describe it; instead, he would define it as a 'radical ethical investment', but of course the condition for such an investment to occur is that the relevant demand is impossible to carry out in the first instance. Secondly, the demand for local and bureaucratic reforms could be considered a particularistic dimension, in the sense of being very specific and concrete and, at the same time, perhaps, relatively feasible. The problem with applying the theory of the empty signifier in this context, however, is that it also supposes a certain 'transference' – specifically, that which occurs in a metaphorical condensation – between the two moments mentioned. Instead, Black Lives Matter's slogan, as we have already explained, is directly perturbing (due to its radical undecidability) and therefore requires people to explain and position themselves politically, over and over again. In our language, the phrase demonstrates the divisiveness of the real of *jouissance*. In other words, its ultimate vocation is to divide, not to condense.

For ourselves, we actually consider the slogan 'Defund the police!' to be a good political example of what in the Lacanian world is called *lalangue*, defined as a way of playing with the dispersed phonemes of language in order to access a *jouissance* that is not entirely present in the established terms, and ordering, of our languages. The prefix 'de-' produced by neologism is the decisive element in this regard. The psychoanalyst Jorge Alemán, in his work, has long advocated *lalangue* as a fundamental element of the political processes of emancipation. We would say that 'Defund the police!' is a very illustrative and interesting example of this idea. Perhaps we have not yet found an adequate categorical nomenclature to describe a demand of this type, beyond its 'lalinguistic' status. We have said that 'empty signifier' is not valid. Calling it a 'radically ambiguous signifier' perhaps does not explain its nuances, either. Surely we will have to find another name. Which simply demonstrates, once again, that politics always moves in advance of (meta-)theory. As Marx said: 'Philosophers have hitherto only interpreted the world in various ways; the point is to change it.' In this sense, the slogan can be said to be a magnificent example of popular political intelligence. Perhaps Black Lives Matters, by deploying it, will transform the world. We hope so.

Note

1 This article was written in the political heat of the George Floyd protests and published on 23 June 2020, in *#lacanemancipa: The Magazine of the Lacanian Left*. A lot has happened in American politics since that time, although the basic theoretical analysis presented here still seems to me to be a valid one. My thanks to my friend Estela Canuto, who helped me very much in the construction and writing of this article.

Chapter 4

Brexit and the tautology of being

The former Prime Minister of Great Britain, Theresa May, will be remembered for very little.[1] Perhaps the most outstanding element of her political discourse was the slogan: 'Brexit means Brexit'.[2] This phrase has produced a great deal of mirth among British liberals, due to its alleged conceptual emptiness. Not for the first time, I disagree with them. Personally, I think that *Brexit means Brexit* is the most coherent political concept that May articulated during her entire period of government. It's certainly better than her other famous phrase: 'We want a red, white and blue Brexit.'[3] It is clear that what May meant, when she stated that *Brexit means Brexit*, was that the Tories were going to go ahead with Britain's exit from the European Union come what may, a promise that helped them win the general election of 2017, albeit without an absolute majority.[4] From my point of view, the phrase is important for another reason: it evokes an important theoretical principle, which could be called *the tautology of being*. What do I mean by this?

In order to understand this idea, I believe we should start with what in philosophy is called an *event*. How should this concept be defined? For my money, the most comprehensive and rigorous definition of it can be found in the work of Alain Badiou.[5] For Badiou, an event is something that comes to supplement what he calls a *situation*, which he defines in terms of an operation that collects and 'counts' a certain set of multiples, thus producing a figure that he calls the *One*. Badiou will add that a situation implies the presence of a *state*. The state, according to him, is an attempt to consolidate a situation by distinguishing the multiples that it already includes from those that it might include in the future. Indirectly, however, this process produces a third category of multiple, which, although it is included in a situation, cannot be said to 'belong' to it. This third category is what Badiou calls a *singularity*. He also calls it 'the eventual site', in the sense that it constitutes a terrain upon which an event may be constructed. However, the fact that an event *may* be erected on the ground of a singular multiple does not mean that it *will* be. A subjective *decision* must also intercede, a decision on whether the multiple in question truly constitutes a singularity or not. To put it in terms of Badiou's 'mathematical ontology', such a process involves deciding that a set can belong to itself, an operation that is prohibited in standard set theory. This, then, is what I call the tautology of being: it means that there not only exists, in the midst of a situation, a singular

DOI: 10.4324/9781003431916-16

multiple, but also that – in violation of all previous norms – it can be identified as such, thus producing an event. I believe that Theresa May's tautology can be interpreted in the same way. *Brexit means Brexit* affirms the very existence of something untoward. Can we therefore deduce that Brexit is an event, in the sense of Badiou? Badiou himself would say not. Why?

It should be remembered that Badiou connects a state of the situation with the political state in the traditional sense. Indeed, this is why he imported the word state into his ontology in the first place. Given, then, that an event is a kind of multiple that only exists by subtracting itself (Badiou's term) from the state of the situation, this implies that no element that has been produced in the ambit of a political state – which corresponds to a state of the situation – can truly be considered an event. This explains the extreme radicalism of Badiou's political positions: according to him, all politics necessarily takes place at a distance from the state. Hence, since Brexit was something that was convoked by the British state, it cannot in any sense be considered an event, according to Badiou's theoretical argument. I have a discrepancy with this conclusion, however. I believe that the Brexit can indeed be called an event, even, up to a certain point, within the theoretical framework set out by Badiou. How so? If one wants to extend the concept of the event (yet without compromising its singularity), it seems to me to be quite clear what one must do. One must delink the state of the situation from the political state. In other words, one must separate Badiou's philosophical theory from his (minimal) social theory. I even believe that Badiou himself does this, in certain symptomatic moments. For example, he uses the political metaphor of the state to talk about moments of relative stability that are found in the other 'conditions' of philosophy that he has identified: art, science and love, even though it should be obvious that, in theoretical terms, these areas have nothing to do with politics. Would it really be so easy, however, to separate the two ontologies? I think it would. In fact, I think that a similar manoeuvre has already been carried out in the work of Jacques Rancière. How does Rancière analyse the political panorama?

Rancière, like Badiou, holds that politics entails the production of a singularity, which he believes will find itself in absolute 'disagreement' (his term) with a certain social *plenum*.[6] The antagonism that Rancière conceives of, at this level, is between what he calls *politics* and *the police*. Couldn't the second of these terms – the police – be considered to be a state in the traditionally political sense, of the kind that had already been denounced by Badiou? Rancière is somewhat ambiguous on the matter, although I would say that in general terms, he does not see it in that way. To put it in Heideggerian terms, the exact 'ontic' form that this 'ontological' category will assume in his work is never entirely specified. I think that a key factor here is that Rancière believes that the proper name of the subject of politics – understood as a force that is opposed to the police – is *the people*. This term is important because it constitutes an absolutely void theoretical category, which allows Rancière to connect it subsequently to concrete political elements that are completely different from one other, and some of which might even constitute segments of what is traditionally called the state. For example, he speaks at a certain point about 'citizens, workers, women, proletarians'.[7] In contrast, Badiou believes that there is only one real emancipatory political subject in action today: the proletariat. This reflects the fact that, for him, there only exists one type of political state in the current situation, which is that of capitalism. Here another question arises, however. If Rancière is more in line with our theoretical position at this level, then why don't we just use his work in order to contemplate Brexit, and do without that of Badiou?

I don't wish to ignore Badiou because I think that there are some nuances in his work that are extremely useful and cannot be found in Rancière. Which ones? First, I think it's important that Badiou views the event in terms of a decision with regard to a social antagonism. I believe this is especially useful if, for example, one wants to discuss *sovereignty*, which I would define in the same way (a definition that would clearly be influenced by the work of Carl Schmitt).[8] I think that sovereignty in this sense is a crucial aspect of the Brexit debate. The second thing that Badiou's project allows us to do, I think, is to contemplate what a subjective adherence to the void of a situation would look like. This is a key dimension of the event, and Badiou opposes it to an adherence to the plenitude of a situation, which would be precisely the function of the state (according to Badiou) or – better – the police (according to Rancière). In fact, Badiou develops a whole theory of this point; he believes that if a subject adheres to a plenitude after glimpsing the void, this is the most regressive form politics that can exist.[9] I believe that this theory allows us to consider a new form of (void) patriotism that is relevant to politics today and can be distinguished from, for example, a certain (plenus) xenophobia, which would constitute a perversion of the former. Once again, I think these factors are also extremely relevant to Brexit. Returning to Rancière, I would say that there is a further absence in his work: he refuses to use the word *populism*. I consider this term important because I think it represents the (philosophical) ideology that corresponds to the aforementioned *people*, which, as I pointed out, should probably be considered the privileged subject of politics. Why does Rancière reject the word? He does so because he believes that it is automatically pejorative, in the political context in which we find ourselves today, above all in Europe.[10] I would accept this point. However, I believe that populism can continue to be of use in our analysis, and also in our praxis. If it is true that I prefer to see things in terms of populism, however, and taking into account that Rancière does not accept the term, why don't I simply refer to the work of those authors who have embraced it openly? Here I have Laclau and Mouffe in mind. What relevance might their work have, in this context?

The difference between the theoretical work of Rancière and Badiou, on the one hand, and Laclau and Mouffe, on the other, is that the former does not deploy the theory of hegemony, while the latter do. Might this concept help us to think about Brexit? After all, if Brexit were considered a hegemonic process, we could perhaps conceive of it as something more politically complex, which might be fruitful in itself. For example, one might conclude that Brexit doesn't only include emancipatory elements – as any event must – but also repressive (or 'transformist', to use the

Gramscian jargon associated with the theory of hegemony) ones, and perhaps such a mixture would provide a more 'realistic' view of the issue. I believe, however, that the theory of hegemony is *too* realistic at this level. What do I mean by this? Essentially, I think that hegemony is good at describing the dispersion of elements in an already-existing social field, but at the cost of diluting its dimension of singularity, which is what I consider to be the essential political aspect. What are the theoretical factors that lead me to this conclusion? I believe that in the end, Laclau and Mouffe are not able, within the scope of their theory, to decide between antagonism in the singular and antagonisms in the plural, and this inevitably undermines the importance of the former. As they themselves say:

> Until now, when we have spoken about antagonism, we have kept it in the singular in order to simplify our argument. But it is clear that antagonism does not necessarily emerge at a single point: any position in a system of differences, insofar as it is negated, can become the locus of an antagonism. Hence, there is a variety of possible antagonisms in the social, many of them in opposition to each other.[11]

Now, on the one hand, this argument could be seen as a useful deconstruction of the 'exclusive singularity' that one finds in projects such as that of Badiou. On the other, it seems to me to be highly politically problematic. Why?

If we want to understand the problem, I think it is necessary to focus on the ambiguous status of the term 'the social' that is referred to in the previous quotation. If it is true, as Laclau and Mouffe have argued on other occasions, that the absolute limit of this social is a singular antagonism, then how can they argue that within the social itself there exist other singular antagonisms? Wouldn't this imply that within the social, understood as the limit of all objectivity, there are other socials, other limits of all objectivity? This would surely be absurd. To put it in other terms, antagonism cannot be and not be at the same time the absolute limit of all objectivity (Russell's paradox haunts us here). A supporter of the theory of hegemony would surely say that this is not truly a problem at all, since the kind of difference that is to be found in a 'system of differences' – an aspect that was also mentioned in the comment by Laclau and Mouffe – is distinct from that which is found in an antagonism *strict sensu*, which constitutes the limit of difference as such. I totally accept this point. But this is not what Laclau and Mouffe are claiming. They are actually arguing that both types of difference can be considered *antagonisms*. I would of course accept that there exist distinct modalities of difference; however, there cannot exist distinct modalities of *antagonism*. If that were the case, then the category would collapse. I think that this ambiguity is what makes it impossible to think the sheer singularity of an antagonism from the perspective of hegemony. Essentially, in the latter theory, singularity is mixed, in an indiscernible way, with plurality. I should perhaps add something here. This conclusion does not imply that for a thinker like Rancière, for example – who I believe is able to think through all the consequences of the category of singularity – there do not exist different political antagonisms. There certainly do, and I have already given examples of them in his work. What it does mean, however, is that such antagonisms do not refer to the same 'social' (in the sense of Laclau and Mouffe). In truth, what Rancière appears to show us is that there are as many social fields as there are social antagonisms, without any possibility of a 'transcendental' combination of either. Nevertheless, and despite the problems that I see with the category of hegemony, I do indeed believe that Laclau and Mouffe should be commended for insisting on the possibility of a populist movement, now understood in terms of a subject who is able to militate in relation to a singular antagonism.

In conclusion, I believe that it is a 'populist' theory – to use the term of Laclau and Mouffe – of the type proposed by Rancière – *qua* 'ontological' radicalisation of the theory of Badiou – that allows us to conclude that Brexit is a singular, and therefore an emancipatory, event within the British political situation. As I have explained, this event is based on a sovereign decision regarding an antagonism, and while there exists the possibility that this decision could subsequently be perverted, thus producing a xenophobic reaction, I do not believe that this 'perversion' is part of the original ontological horizon of this decision (which is what the theory of hegemony would have to assume). To put it in the terms of a lesser theorist, Theresa May, I think we can indeed conclude that *Brexit means Brexit*.

Notes

1 This article was first published in the following journal: Timothy Appleton, Brexit and the Tautology of Being, *Filozofski vestnik*, Vol. 40, No. 2, 2019.
2 www.independent.co.uk/news/uk/politics/theresa-may-brexit-means-brexit-conservative-leadership-no-attempt-remain-inside-eu-leave-europe-a7130596.html.
3 www.bbc.com/news/av/38223990/theresa-may-we-want-a-red-white-and-blue-brexit.
4 And which completely demolished the opposition in the general election of 2019.
5 Alain Badiou, *Being and Event* (London: Continuum), 2005.
6 Jacques Rancière, *Disagreement* (Minnesota: University of Minnesota), 1999.
7 Jacques Rancière, *Disagreement* (Minnesota: University of Minnesota), 1999, p. 59.
8 Carl Schmitt, *Political Theology – Four Chapters on the Concept of Sovereignty* (Chicago: University of Chicago), 2005. See also, Carl Schmitt, *The Concept of the Political* (Chicago: University of Chicago), 2007, p. 49.
9 See: Alain Badiou, *Ethics – An Essay on the Understanding of Evil* (London: Verso), 2001.
10 Alain Badiou, Pierre Bourdieu, Judith Butler, Georges Didi Huberman, Sadri Khiari and Jacques Rancière, *What Is a People?* (New York: Columbia University Press), 2013, pp. 101–105.
11 Ernesto Laclau and Chantal Mouffe, *Hegemony and Socialist Strategy – Towards a Radical Democratic Politics* (London: Verso), 1985, p. 131.

Index

Note: Page numbers in *italics* indicate a figure.

For Product Safety Concerns and Information please contact our EU
representative GPSR@taylorandfrancis.com
Taylor & Francis Verlag GmbH, Kaufingerstraße 24, 80331 München, Germany